◆ EDIBLE PARTY ◆
Bouquets

Creating Gifts and Centerpieces
with Fruit, Appetizers, and Desserts

FOX CHAPEL
PUBLISHING

ISBN 978-1-56523-723-0

642.8

To learn more about the other great books from Fox Chapel Publishing, or to find a retailer near you, call toll free 800-457-9112 or visit us at *www.FoxChapelPublishing.com*.

Note to Authors: We are always looking for talented authors to write new books. Please send a brief letter describing your idea to Acquisition Editor, 1970 Broad Street, East Petersburg, PA 17520.

Printed in China
First printing

Introduction

Next time you're invited to a party, make an impression by bringing one of these interesting and easy-to-make edible bouquets. With the help of this book, you'll achieve professional-looking results with ease.

For those of you expected to produce the crudités for a gathering, try one of the vegetable arrangements—Regal Relishes (page 94) will do the trick. If you prefer a sweeter flavor, there are a variety of fruit recipes, as well as more decadent choices that include cookies, candies, pies, cupcakes, and more. If you can't decide whether to be healthy or not, take the middle road and arrange a bouquet with chocolate-dipped berries and fruit. There are even heartier options featuring meats, cheeses, and breads, such as the BLT Bouquet (page 116) and Pinwheel Palooza (page 119).

No matter which recipe you select, one thing is certain—your bouquet will be fresh, delicious, and the star of the party. Happy arranging!

Contents

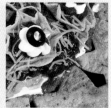

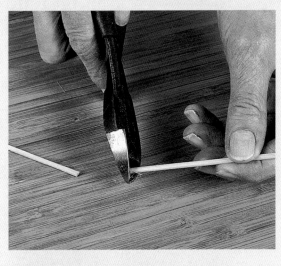

Getting Started

Serving appetizers and snacks is a great way to begin any get-together, and when you display them as beautiful centerpieces or bouquets, guests will admire your handiwork as they mingle around the table. To create that special centerpiece, just whip up an easy-to-make fruit bouquet that is both incredible and edible!

Add the finishing touch to a special meal with a dessert that serves double-duty as an edible centerpiece or bouquet. Every meal deserves dessert, but a dessert bouquet shows guests you care. These bouquets also make a unique and greatly appreciated homemade gift.

Our photos and step-by-step instructions make it easy to turn ordinary treats into extraordinary displays. So, why just make an appetizer, snack, or dessert? Make it extra special with an Edible Party Bouquet!

Practice Food Safety

Before you begin any food project, wash your hands with soap and warm water thoroughly and often while handling food. Make sure your work surface is clean and sanitary. Use well-sharpened knives properly with a cutting board underneath and practice general kitchen safety when handling sharp utensils.

Choose the freshest foods available and always wash them. Under running water, rub fruits and vegetables briskly with your hands to remove dirt and surface microorganisms and be sure to pat dry with paper towels before using. Prior to cutting or peeling fruits and vegetables such as melons, carrots, or pineapples, scrub the outer hard rind or firm skin under running water with a vegetable brush. Waxes are often applied to produce such as apples, cucumbers, and zucchini to help retain moisture. So do not wash these fruits and vegetables until you are ready to create your fruit bouquets in order to keep them firm and crisp as long as possible. To keep sliced vegetables fresh and crisp until bouquet assembly, soak them in ice water for 15 minutes or cover with damp paper towels.

It is important to keep most fruits and vegetables cool while preparing and arranging your bouquet. After pieces of the bouquet are cut, refrigerate them as directed until ready to assemble the bouquet. For optimal freshness and beauty, serve bouquets promptly after assembly. If holding time in a refrigerator is required, do not add bread items like breadsticks, crackers, and pretzels until just before serving. It is recommended that your bouquet be displayed and served the same day it is prepared. Bouquets made from fresh fruit should be kept cool and served shortly after assembly or stored for a short time, loosely covered, in the refrigerator. Some bouquets, such as those made from chocolate, need to be kept cool to prevent melting. Store them in a cool location out of direct sunlight.

If you intend to display your bouquet as a centerpiece, assemble and serve it as close to the beginning of the event as possible. If your bouquet needs to be transported, cover it loosely with a large food-safe plastic bag and pack it securely in a large cooler. If the bouquet is a gift, encourage the recipient to enjoy the produce as quickly as possible and to store any leftovers tightly covered in the refrigerator, removing non-perishable bread items first to prevent sogginess.

GATHER SOME GENERAL SUPPLIES

These supplies can be purchased in kitchen shops, grocery stores and the craft or baking section of most discount stores:

- ❏ Wooden or bamboo skewers, white lollipop or cookie sticks, plastic hors d'oeuvre picks, etc.
- ❏ Round and flat toothpicks
- ❏ Styrofoam ("foam")
- ❏ Knife for trimming foam
- ❏ Food-safe containers, plates and platters
- ❏ Parchment paper, plastic wrap, waxed paper, and aluminum foil
- ❏ Cutting boards
- ❏ Knives, such as chef's, paring, serrated, etc.
- ❏ Crinkle cutter
- ❏ Cookie cutters (metal and plastic)
- ❏ Melon baller
- ❏ Scissors and pizza cutter
- ❏ Pruning shears
- ❏ Pastry bags fitted with decorative tips
- ❏ Rolling pin
- ❏ Rimmed baking sheets
- ❏ Nonstick cooking spray
- ❏ Ribbons, raffia, and other embellishments
- ❏ Tape
- ❏ Tissue paper
- ❏ Heavy-duty zippered plastic bags
- ❏ Food coloring (Gel or paste coloring is recommended for the best color and consistency.)

Prepare the Base

Choosing a container for your dessert bouquet is an important consideration. It should be attractive, sturdy, and appropriately sized for your bouquet. The container can sometimes be painted or covered in paper to fit the theme and color of your bouquet.

When directions call for a non-edible Styrofoam base, purchase a piece of foam that most closely matches the container's size and shape. If it still needs trimming, simply press the container's opening against the foam to make an outline. Cut with a knife, about a half-inch inside the outline. Trim foam as needed so it fits into container with a little space to spare. Generally, the height of the foam should be about one inch shorter than the top of the container, unless directed differently for a specific bouquet.

Wrap foam in aluminum foil to prevent contact with food. Test the fit again; covered foam should fit snugly in container for a stable and secure bouquet. The foil can be disguised by arranging another food over the top, such as nuts, coffee beans, or leafy greens like kale.

In some bouquets, a food product may be used inside the container for the base. This might include an item that can be eaten, such as a pan of bars or a pineapple, or it might be a product that will not be consumed, such as the shell of a melon or a head of lettuce.

A head of iceberg lettuce is a great, inexpensive way to secure fruit flowers in a bouquet. It can be easily cut to size to fit most containers. For large containers, you might use more than one head. For small containers, lettuce can be torn into large pieces and layered in the container. Cabbage is not recommended as a base since the surface is hard to puncture.

Plan your arrangements based on the size of your container and the number of guests you plan to serve. Use the photos for ideas and then personalize your bouquets by choosing skewer lengths and placements that work for you. Think about the season or party theme when choosing containers and pick colors that complement the appetizers, snacks, or desserts.

Place the Foods

A variety of skewers can be used to display foods—plain or frill toothpicks, bamboo or plastic cocktail picks and white lollipop or cookie sticks. Common wooden or bamboo skewers, 10-to-12 inches long, are inexpensive, versatile, and easy to find. They can be trimmed to desired lengths with sanitary pruning shears. They can also be inserted into green onion stems to resemble real flower stems.

In most cases, it's best to slide food onto the pointed end of a skewer and poke the blunt end into the base, unless directed otherwise. If necessary, make starter holes with a toothpick or skewer point. Some foods tend to slide down a long skewer after assembly. To prevent this, place a "stopper," such as a raisin or small piece of bell pepper, on the skewer before adding the appetizers.

Ten-inch bamboo skewers are recommended for flower stems. They are inexpensive, widely available, and easy to cut if necessary. To prevent sliding, wrap small craft rubber bands approximately two inches from the pointed end of a skewer to make a ridge. If you prefer a food item, use a raisin or gumdrop.

Sweet

Pretty in Pink, page 61.

Dipp'n Dots, page 18.

Truffle Tower, page 58.

Basket of Daisies

A refreshing combination of juicy fruits in a basket

You Will Need:

- 2 to 3 whole fresh pineapples
- 1 small cantaloupe
- 1 small bunch green grapes
- Flower-shaped metal cookie cutters
- Melon baller

- 20 to 25 (10") bamboo skewers
- 1 head iceberg lettuce
- 1 small bunch purple or green kale or leafy lettuce
- 1 medium oval basket

1 Begin by slicing a pineapple sideways into ¾"- to 1"-disks. Cut the pineapple over a sheet pan with a rimmed edge to catch the juice. For a medium-size bouquet, you will need 13 to 15 pineapple disks. To cut the flowers, center one of the flower-shaped cookie cutters over a pineapple disk. (Metal cookie cutters are recommended for a clean, even cut.) Press straight down on the cookie cutter, using even pressure.

2 Turn the pineapple disk over and gently press the flower shape out of the disk. Cut the remaining disks into flowers using various sizes of flower-shaped cookie cutters. Place the pineapple flowers in an even layer on a clean rimmed baking sheet; place in the refrigerator to chill while assembling the remaining pieces. Any remaining pieces of the cut pineapple disks can be discarded.

3 To make the flower centers, cut the cantaloupe in half and remove the seeds. Using a melon baller, cut balls from the orange cantaloupe flesh. The balls can be either completely round or they can have one slightly flat side. Cut enough balls to have one for the center of each pineapple flower. Place the cantaloupe balls on a plate and refrigerate to chill while assembling the grape spears.

4 To make the grape spears, thread 4 or 5 similar-size grapes onto a wooden skewer, starting at the stem-side of each grape and piercing straight through to the bottom end of each grape. Do not pierce all the way through the final grape on each spear, allowing the skewer to remain concealed. For a medium-size bouquet, you will need 6 to 8 grape spears. Place the grape spears on a plate and refrigerate to chill while assembling the base.

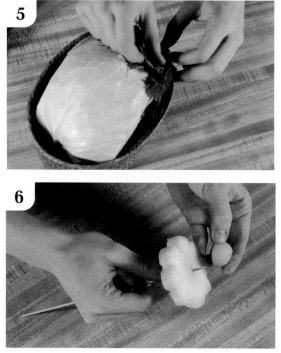

5 While the fruit pieces are chilling, prepare the lettuce base. Cut the head of lettuce as necessary to fit easily into the basket. For a medium oval-shaped basket, such as that used in the photo, cut about 1½" from both sides of the lettuce head. If necessary, use the cut-off pieces to fill the bottom of the basket. Place the lettuce head in the basket so the top of the lettuce sits 1" to 2" above the rim of the basket. Stick purple or green kale leaves into the basket around the lettuce. Continue adding kale until the lettuce is completely covered. The skewers of fruit added later will hold the kale in place.

6 To assemble the daisies, remove the pineapple flowers and cantaloupe centers from the refrigerator. Pierce the hard center of one pineapple flower with a skewer, pressing from the bottom side of the flower, through the center, to the top side of the flower, allowing about ½" of the skewer to be exposed on the top side. Press one cantaloupe ball onto the exposed

end of the skewer, stopping before the skewer pierces the top end of the ball. If necessary, use rubber bands, gumdrops or raisins to keep the flowers from sliding down the skewers, as explained on page 9.

7 Arrange the daisies in the basket, starting with the bigger blooms around the bottom and filling in with the smaller blooms as the arrangement fills up. Pierce the skewers through the kale and into the lettuce until the flowers sit at desired height. If necessary, cut the skewers down to an appropriate height using nail clippers.

8 As the basket is filling with daisies, carefully stick the grape spears into the arrangement to fill any gaps. When you are happy with your bouquet, carefully package it for delivery or return the entire arrangement to the refrigerator until ready to display and serve.

Sweet Kisses

A hearty burst of sweetness for that special event

You Will Need:

- ❑ 1 whole pineapple
- ❑ 25 to 30 strawberries
- ❑ 8 to 10 caramel-filled chocolate kisses
- ❑ Heart-shaped metal cookie cutters
- ❑ 30 to 40 (10") bamboo skewers

- ❑ 1 head iceberg lettuce
- ❑ 1 small bunch purple or green kale or leafy lettuce
- ❑ 1 large vase, ceramic planter or urn

1 Begin by slicing a pineapple sideways into ¾"- to 1"-disks. Cut the pineapple over a sheet pan with a rimmed edge to catch the juice. For a medium-size bouquet, you will need 6 to 8 pineapple disks. To cut the hearts, center one of the heart-shaped cookie cutters over a pineapple disk. (Metal cookie cutters are recommended for a clean, even cut.) Press straight down on the cookie cutter, using even pressure.

2 Turn the pineapple disk over and gently press the heart shape out of the disk. Cut the remaining disks into hearts using various sizes of heart-shaped cookie cutters. Place the pineapple hearts in an even layer on a clean rimmed baking sheet; place in the refrigerator to chill while assembling the remaining pieces. Any remaining pieces of the cut pineapple disks can be discarded.

3 Next, create the strawberry buds. Rinse the strawberries under cool water and pat dry gently with paper towels. Choose large, full strawberries of a similar size. If desired, remove the stem and leaves from each strawberry, however it is not necessary to do so. Poke the pointed end of a skewer into the stem end of a strawberry, stopping before the skewer pierces through the berry; repeat with remaining berries and skewers, then refrigerate. If desired, skewers can hold two, three or even four strawberries for added height.

4 For a large, tall vase, such as that used in the photo, it is necessary to fill up the bottom of the vase with material before inserting the lettuce base. Place tightly-packed folded kitchen towels in the vase until it is a little more than halfway full. If you do not want to use towels, the base can be filled with cut-to-size Styrofoam or additional lettuce pieces.

5 Once the vase is more than halfway full, cut the lettuce head to fit in the vase. Place the lettuce head in the vase so the top of the lettuce sits about 1" above the rim of the vase. Stick purple or green kale leaves around and over top of the lettuce to cover. The skewers of fruit added later will hold the kale in place.

6 To assemble the bouquet, begin by inserting a skewer into the pointed side of each pineapple heart. Slide the heart vertically down onto the skewer until the skewer hits the hard center of the pineapple piece. Next, place the hearts in the bouquet. Do this by piercing the bottom end of the skewer through the kale and into the lettuce base. Place the larger hearts near the center and the smaller hearts on either side.

7 Once all the pineapple hearts are in place, stick the strawberry buds into the bouquet to fill any gaps. Place the buds close together, in order to cover as much of the kale as possible. Turn the vase often while arranging to make sure it is filled evenly on all sides. Sometimes, it is easier to place the strawberry buds in the bouquet by first sticking a skewer into the kale and then sliding the strawberry onto the skewer.

8 Add the final touch by garnishing the arrangement with kiss blossoms. Carefully stick the pointed end of a skewer into the bottom flat side of one chocolate kiss; repeat with the remaining kisses and skewers. Stick the kiss blossoms into the small spaces between the pineapple hearts and strawberry buds.

Dipp'n Dots

Sweet, fruity, and saucy in a fondue style

You Will Need:

- ❏ 2 clementines
- ❏ 2 bananas
- ❏ 1 pint blueberries
- ❏ 1 pint raspberries
- ❏ 1 small bunch green and/or purple grapes
- ❏ 20 to 25 (10") bamboo skewers
- ❏ 1 head iceberg lettuce
- ❏ 1 small to medium tall canister

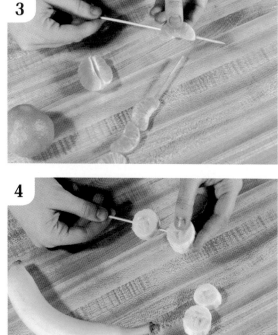

1 Begin by making the grape spears. Thread 5 or 6 similar-size grapes onto a skewer, starting at the stem-side of each grape and piercing straight through to the bottom end of each grape. Do not pierce all the way through the final grape on each spear, allowing the skewer to remain concealed. For a small-size bouquet, you will need about 10 grape spears. Place the grape spears on a plate and refrigerate to chill while assembling the remaining spears.

2 To make the blueberry spears, thread 8 to 10 similar-size blueberries onto a skewer, starting at the bottom of each berry and piercing straight through to the top end. Do not pierce all the way through the final berry on each spear. For a small-size bouquet, you will need 4 to 6 blueberry spears. Create about 5 raspberry spears in the same fashion, threading the berries upside down onto the skewers. Place the berry spears on a plate and refrigerate to chill.

3 Peel the Clementines and divide the fruit into sections, removing any white membrane or pith from the sections. To make the Clementine spears, thread 4 or 5 sections vertically onto a skewer, alternating the direction each section faces. For a small-size bouquet, you will need 3 to 5 Clementine spears. Place the spears on a plate and refrigerate to chill.

4 Peel the bananas and cut them into ½" rounds. Dip in lemon juice and pat dry with paper towels. Thread 4 or 5 rounds onto a skewer, starting at the side of each round and piercing straight through to the other side. Do not pierce all the way through the final banana round on each spear. For a small-size bouquet, you will need 3 to 5 banana spears. Set aside the banana spears until ready to assemble the bouquet.

5 Next, prepare the lettuce base. Cut the head of lettuce into round thick pieces and layer them into the canister. Fill the canister ¾ full with tightly-packed lettuce. Do not extend the lettuce above the rim since the spears will be stuck down into the canister. If desired, cover the lettuce pieces with green or purple kale.

6 Remove all the spears from the refrigerator and arrange them in the canister, alternating different fruit types. Turn the canister often while arranging to make sure it is filled evenly on all sides. Place the shorter skewers around the edge with the taller skewers in the middle. When you are happy with your bouquet, carefully package it for delivery or return the entire arrangement to the refrigerator until ready to display and serve.

CHOCOLATE DIPPING SAUCE

Add the final touch to your Dipp'n Dots bouquet by presenting it with this fondue-style chocolate sauce. It is so easy to make and will stay at a good dipping consistency for about 45 minutes. To re-melt the sauce, simply microwave it for 20 seconds and stir.

Ingredients
- ½ C. butter
- 1 (14 oz.) can sweetened condensed milk
- 6 to 8 oz. chocolate chips

Directions
In a medium saucepan over low heat, combine the butter, sweetened condensed milk and chocolate chips. Heat, stirring often, until the mixture is completely melted and smooth. Make sure to keep the heat low, as the sauce burns easily. Transfer the chocolate sauce to a serving dish. Place it on the table alongside the fruit bouquet and encourage guests to dip their fruit pieces into the sauce.

Melon Mania

A crazy combo of popular melon varieties

You Will Need:

- ❏ 1 small to medium watermelon
- ❏ 1 to 2 cantaloupes
- ❏ 1 to 2 honeydew melons
- ❏ Flower-shaped metal cookie cutters
- ❏ Melon baller
- ❏ Crinkle cutter

- ❏ 15 to 20 (10") bamboo skewers
- ❏ 1 head iceberg lettuce
- ❏ 1 small bunch purple or green kale or leafy lettuce
- ❏ 1 medium wide-mouth vase or urn

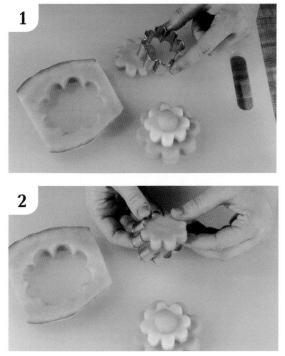

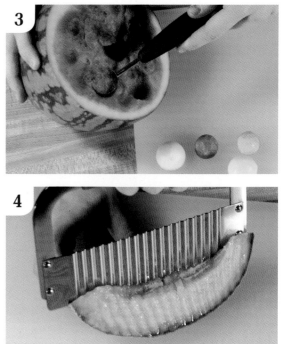

1 Begin by slicing the watermelon, cantaloupe and honeydew melons sideways into ¾"- to 1"-disks. Cut the melons over a sheet pan with a rimmed edge to catch the juice. For a medium-size bouquet, you will need 16 to 20 various melon disks. To cut the flowers, center one of the flower-shaped cookie cutters over a melon disk. (Metal cookie cutters are recommended for a clean, even cut.) Press straight down on the cookie cutter, using even pressure.

2 Cut small-, medium- and large-size flowers out of each type of melon. Turn the melon disks over and gently press the flower shapes out of the disks. Place the melon flowers in an even layer on a clean rimmed baking sheet; place in the refrigerator to chill while assembling the remaining pieces.

3 Use the remaining pieces of watermelon, cantaloupe and honeydew melon to make the flower centers. Cut balls from the melon flesh using a melon baller. The balls can be either completely round or they can have one slightly flat side. For a medium-size bouquet, you will need 8 to 10 flower centers. Place the melon balls on a plate and refrigerate to chill while assembling the melon leaves.

4 Next, cut the melon leaves. You will need half of a cantaloupe and half of a honeydew melon to make enough leaves for a medium-size bouquet. Cut the melons into wedges that measure about 1" to 1½" on the widest side. If a rippled effect is desired, cut the melon wedges using a crinkle cutter, as shown. Run a knife as close to the outer edge of the melon flesh as possible in order to remove the rind. Refrigerate the melon leaves.

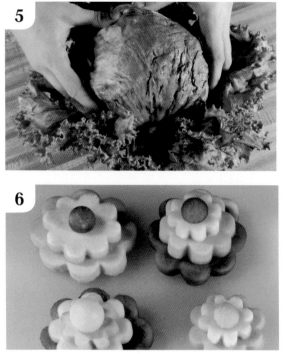

5 Next, prepare the lettuce base. Cut the head of lettuce as necessary to fit easily into the vase. Place the lettuce head in the vase so the top of the lettuce sits 1" to 2" above the rim of the vase. Stick purple or green kale leaves into the basket to cover the lettuce. The skewers of fruit added later will hold the kale in place.

6 Stack various sizes and colors of melon flowers to create multiple looks. Pierce the center of one large base flower, pressing from the bottom side, through the center, to the top side of the flower. Slide a smaller flower down onto the skewer so it sits on top of the base flower. If desired, top with another smaller flower. If necessary, use rubber bands, gumdrops or raisins to keep the flowers from sliding down the skewers, as explained on page 9.

7 Continue sliding the flowers down the skewer until about ½" of the skewer is exposed on the top side. Press one melon ball onto the exposed end of the skewer. Then, arrange the melon flowers in the vase. Pierce the skewers through the kale and into the lettuce until the flowers sit at desired height. Sometimes, it is easier to place the melon flowers in the bouquet by first sticking skewers into the kale and then sliding the melon flowers and melon balls onto the skewers.

8 As the vase is filling with flowers, carefully slide the melon leaves onto skewers. Stick the skewers into the arrangement around the rim of the vase. When you are happy with your bouquet, carefully package it for delivery or return the entire arrangement to the refrigerator until ready to display and serve.

Autumn Apples

Fall into this seasonal favorite, with classic caramel sauce

You Will Need:

- ❏ 6 to 10 various-colored apples
- ❏ Crinkle cutter
- ❏ 20 to 30 (10") bamboo skewers
- ❏ 1 head iceberg lettuce
- ❏ 1 small bunch purple or green kale or leafy lettuce
- ❏ 1 medium wide-mouth vase or urn

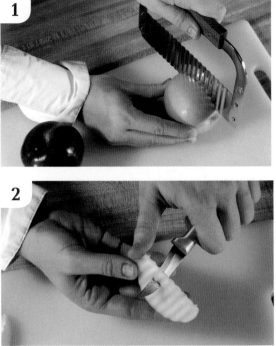

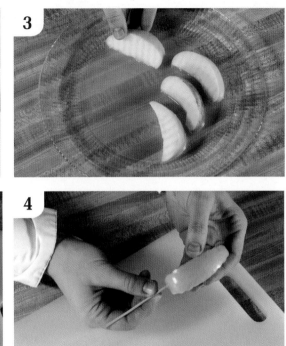

1 Begin by slicing the apples into wedges. Choose apples of various color and sweetness. For the display shown, Red Delicious, Golden Delicious, Granny Smith and Gala apples were used. Other appropriate apples to use are: Ambrosia, Braeburn, Criterion, Ginger Gold, Honeycrisp and Pink Lady.

2 If a rippled effect is desired, cut the apple wedges using a crinkle cutter, as shown above. Cut each apple into approximately 6 to 8 wedges, depending on your desired thickness. For a medium-size bouquet, you will need 50 to 60 apple wedges. Once all the wedges are cut, use a paring knife to cut away any of the core, seeds or stem still attached to the apples.

3 To keep the apples from browning, place them immediately on a plate and sprinkle them with lemon juice. Allow the wedges to sit in the juice for about 30 seconds, then turn each wedge over and sprinkle them again. After 1 minute, transfer the apples to a clean plate and set aside.

4 Break each skewer in half so you have approximately 40 to 60 (5") skewers. Short skewers are desirable since the apple wedges sit close to the base. Insert one short skewer into one pointed end of each apple wedge. Press the skewers 1½" to 2" vertically into the apple wedges. Place the skewered apples back on the plate and set aside while assembling the lettuce base.

5 Next, prepare the lettuce base. Cut the head of lettuce as necessary to fit easily into the vase. Place the lettuce head in the vase so the top of the lettuce sits 1" to 2" above the rim of the vase. Stick purple or green kale leaves into the vase to cover the lettuce. The skewers of fruit added later will hold the kale in place.

6 Finally, arrange the apple skewers in the vase, alternating types and colors of apples. Stick the skewers into the arrangement in rows around the rim of the vase. Continue filling the bouquet, turning the vase often while arranging to make sure it is filled evenly on all sides. When you are happy with your bouquet, carefully package it for delivery or return the entire arrangement to the refrigerator until ready to display and serve.

CARAMEL DIPPING SAUCE

The only thing that could make crisp, juicy apples even sweeter is this decadent caramel dipping sauce. Serve or give it with your Autumn Apples bouquet for a crowd-pleasing presentation. To soften the caramel sauce, simply microwave it for 20 seconds and stir.

Ingredients

- ½ C. butter
- 1 (14 oz.) bag caramels, unwrapped
- 1 (14 oz.) can sweetened condensed milk

Directions

In a medium saucepan over low heat, combine the butter, caramels and sweetened condensed milk. Heat, stirring often, until the mixture is completely melted and smooth. Make sure to keep the heat low, as the sauce burns easily. Transfer the caramel sauce to a serving dish. Place it on the table alongside the fruit bouquet and encourage guests to dip their apple wedges into the sauce.

Catching Snowflakes

Make a winter wonderland of fruits any time of year

You Will Need:

- ❑ 17 to 20 strawberries
- ❑ 2 to 3 kiwis
- ❑ 1 pineapple
- ❑ 1 small bunch purple grapes
- ❑ Miniature marshmallows
- ❑ Snowflake-shaped metal cookie cutter

- ❑ 35 to 40 (10") bamboo skewers
- ❑ 1 head iceberg lettuce
- ❑ 1 small bunch purple or green kale or leafy lettuce
- ❑ 1 (6" tall) decorative metal bucket

1 Begin by slicing the pineapple sideways into ¾"- to 1"-disks. Cut the pineapple over a sheet pan with a rimmed edge to catch the juice. For a medium- size bouquet, you will need 4 to 6 pineapple disks. To cut the snowflakes, center the snowflake-shaped cookie cutter over a pineapple disk. (Metal cookie cutters are recommended for a clean, even cut.) Press straight down on the cookie cutter, using even pressure.

2 Turn the pineapple disk over and gently press the snowflake shape out of the disk. Cut the remaining disks into snowflakes and place them in an even layer on a clean rimmed baking sheet. Insert a skewer into the crevice between two points of the pineapple snowflake. Slide the snowflake vertically down onto the skewer until the skewer hits the hard center of the pineapple piece. Refrigerate the snowflakes while assembling the remaining pieces. Any remaining pieces of the cut pineapple disks can be discarded.

3 To make the grape-mallow spears, alternately thread grapes and miniature marshmallows onto a wooden skewer, starting and ending with a grape. Do not pierce all the way through the final grape on each spear, allowing the skewer to remain concealed. For a medium-size bouquet, you will need about 6 grape-mallow spears. Place the spears on a plate and refrigerate to chill.

4 Cut each kiwi in half to make the kiwi flowers. Using a paring knife, gently peel and discard the outer brown skin from each kiwi half. Stick a skewer into the thickest part of each kiwi half, pressing into the rounded side and stopping before the skewer pierces through the flat side of the kiwi. If necessary, use rubber bands, gumdrops or raisins to keep the flowers from sliding down the skewers, as explained on page 9. Place the kiwi flowers on a plate and refrigerate.

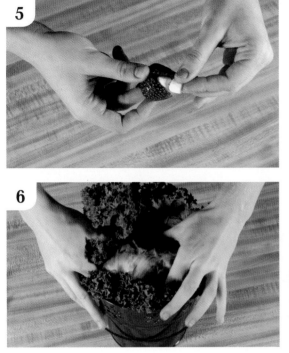

5 To make the strawberry-mallow blossoms, rinse the strawberries under cool water and pat dry gently with paper towels. Choose large, full strawberries of a similar size. If desired, remove the stem and leaves from each strawberry, however it is not necessary to do so. Cut a slit ⅔ of the way into each strawberry, starting at the pointed end. Stick a skewer into each berry from the stem end. Slide 1 or 2 miniature marshmallows onto the exposed end of each skewer.

6 Next, prepare the lettuce base. Cut the head of lettuce as necessary to fit easily into the bucket. Place the lettuce head in the bucket so the top of the lettuce sits 1" to 2" above the rim of the bucket. Stick purple or green kale leaves into the bucket to cover the lettuce. The skewers of fruit added later will hold the kale in place.

7 Remove all the fruit pieces from the refrigerator and start arranging the fruit flowers in the bucket. Place the pineapple snowflakes first, followed by the strawberry-mallow blossoms. Once most of the strawberries are in place, arrange the kiwi flowers in the bucket, flat side facing up.

8 As the basket is filling with flowers, carefully stick the grape-mallow spears into the arrangement to fill any gaps. Turn the bucket often while arranging to make sure it is filled evenly on all sides. When you are happy with your bouquet, carefully package it for delivery or return the entire arrangement to the refrigerator until ready to display and serve.

Shooting Star

Melons and berries topped with a shining pineapple star

You Will Need:

- 1 whole pineapple (just 1 disk needed)
- 1 pint blueberries
- 8 to 10 strawberries
- ½ honeydew melon
- ½ cantaloupe
- Star-shaped metal cookie cutter
- 25 to 30 (10") bamboo skewers
- 1 head iceberg lettuce
- 1 small bunch purple or green kale or leafy lettuce
- 1 medium vase, ceramic planter or urn

1 Begin by cutting one ¾"- to 1"-disk from the pineapple. Use the remaining pineapple for other purposes. To cut the star, center the star-shaped cookie cutter over the pineapple disk. (Metal cookie cutters are recommended for a clean, even cut.) Press straight down on the cookie cutter, using even pressure.

2 Turn the pineapple disk over and gently press the star shape out of the disk. Any remaining pieces of the cut pineapple disks can be discarded. Insert a skewer into the crevice between two points of the pineapple star. Slide the star vertically down onto the skewer until the skewer hits the hard center of the pineapple piece. Set the pineapple star on a clean plate; place in the refrigerator to chill while assembling the remaining pieces.

3 Next, make the blueberry spears. Thread 6 to 8 similar-size blueberries onto a wooden skewer, starting at the bottom-side of each blueberry and piercing straight through to the top end of each berry. Do not pierce all the way through the final berry on each spear, allowing the skewer to remain concealed. For a medium-size bouquet, you will need 8 to 10 blueberry spears. Place the berry spears on a plate and refrigerate to chill while assembling the base.

4 To create the strawberry buds, rinse the strawberries under cool water and pat dry gently with paper towels. Choose large, full strawberries of a similar size. If desired, remove the stem and leaves from each strawberry, however it is not necessary to do so. Poke the pointed end of a skewer into the stem end of a strawberry, stopping before the skewer pierces through the berry; repeat with remaining berries and skewers, then refrigerate.

5 Next, cut the melon leaves. You will need half of a cantaloupe and half of a honeydew melon to make enough leaves for a medium-size bouquet. Cut the melons into wedges that measure about 1" to 1½" on the widest side. If a rippled effect is desired, cut the melon wedges using a crinkle cutter. Run a knife as close to the outer edge of the melon flesh as possible in order to remove the rind. Finally, cut each wedge in half to make two leaves. Refrigerate the melon leaves.

6 Prepare the lettuce base. Cut the head of lettuce as necessary to fit easily into the urn. Place the lettuce head in the urn so the top of the lettuce sits 1" to 2" above the rim of the urn. Stick purple or green kale leaves into the urn to cover the lettuce. The skewers of fruit added later will hold the kale in place.

7 Begin arranging the fruit pieces in the urn. Carefully slide the melon leaves onto skewers. Place a row of melon leaves around the rim of the urn, curved side facing down, alternating between cantaloupe and honeydew melon leaves. Stick the strawberry buds into the urn in a circle just inside the row of melon leaves.

8 Slide about 6 blueberries onto the skewer holding the pineapple star in order to conceal the skewer. Stick the pineapple star into the center of the bouquet. Surround the star with desired amount of blueberry spears. When you are happy with your bouquet, carefully package it for delivery or return the entire arrangement to the refrigerator until ready to display and serve.

Citrus Smiles

Put on a happy face with pears, oranges, grapes and strawberries

You Will Need:

- ❏ 1 pear
- ❏ 1 small bunch purple globe grapes
- ❏ 3 to 4 clementines
- ❏ 1 to 2 large oranges
- ❏ 6 to 8 strawberries
- ❏ 20 to 30 (10") bamboo skewers
- ❏ 1 head iceberg lettuce
- ❏ 1 small bunch purple or green kale or leafy lettuce
- ❏ 1 medium ceramic canister or jar

1 Begin by creating the strawberry buds. Rinse the strawberries under cool water and pat dry gently with paper towels. Choose large, full strawberries of a similar size. If desired, remove the stem and leaves from each strawberry, however it is not necessary to do so. Poke the pointed end of a skewer into the stem end of a strawberry stopping before the skewer pierces through the berry; repeat with remaining berries and skewers, then refrigerate.

2 Peel the oranges and Clementines, then use a paring knife to remove as much of the white pith as possible. Gently separate the oranges and Clementines into halves. Set aside one of the orange halves and two of the Clementine halves. Separate the remaining oranges and Clementines into individual segments.

3 Next, create several styles of orange and Clementine spears. Make sailboat spears by sliding two Clementine segments sideways onto a skewer so the segments form a boat shape. Create several tall spears by sliding orange segments vertically onto a skewer. Finally, make a few Clementine-grape spears by alternately sliding Clementine segments and grapes onto a skewer.

4 Use the reserved orange and Clementine halves to create the citrus blossoms. Set a single grape in the indentation of one orange half, pressing down lightly on the grape. Press a skewer into the orange from the bottom, through the grape, then back into the orange flesh so the flat side of the orange is facing forward and the grape is secured into the center of the orange. Repeat with the remaining Clementine halves. For a medium-size bouquet, you will need 3 to 5 citrus blossoms.

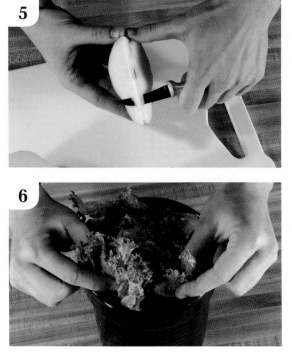

5 Gently rinse the pear under cool water. Cut the pear into 6 even segments. Use a paring knife to cut a shallow curve into the pear removing the core area and any seeds. Dip in lemon juice and pat dry with paper towels. Set a single grape in the indentation of one pear segment. Holding the grape in place, stick a skewer into the pear segment from the bottom end through the grape and back into the pear flesh so the pear is sitting vertically and the grape is secured in the center groove of the pear.

6 Next, prepare the lettuce base. Cut the head of lettuce as necessary to fit easily into the canister. Place the lettuce head in the canister so the top of the lettuce sits 1" to 2" above the rim of the canister. Stick purple or green kale leaves into the canister to cover the lettuce. The skewers of fruit added later will hold the kale in place.

7 Start arranging the fruit by placing several sailboat spears around the rim of the canister. Place a row of strawberry buds behind the sailboat spears. Arrange the pear segments around the bouquet, turning the canister often while arranging to make sure it is filled evenly on all sides. Stick the orange and Clementine halves into the arrangement, as well as the Clementine-grape spears.

8 If a playful look is desired, the pieces can be arranged to resemble a smiley face, with the Clementine halves placed as eyes and the sailboat spears placed as a mouth, similar to the arrangement on page 33. When you are happy with your bouquet, carefully package it for delivery or return the entire arrangement to the refrigerator until ready to display and serve.

Feelin' Fruity

A splash of chocolate coating dresses up this burst of melon, citrus, and berry favorites

You Will Need:

- ❑ 1 personal-size small watermelon
- ❑ 1 whole pineapple
- ❑ 1 large orange
- ❑ 10 to 12 strawberries
- ❑ 1 small bunch purple grapes
- ❑ ½ cantaloupe
- ❑ ½ honeydew melon
- ❑ Flower-shaped cookie cutters and melon baller

- ❑ 1 (16 oz.) pkg. microwaveable chocolate candy coating
- ❑ 12" disposable decorating bag with optional small tip (#3)
- ❑ 25 to 35 (10") bamboo skewers
- ❑ 1 head iceberg lettuce
- ❑ 1 small bunch purple or green kale or leafy lettuce

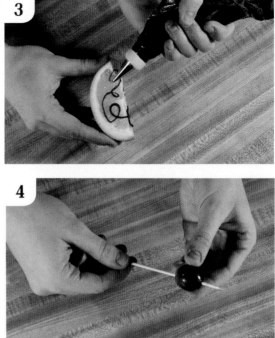

1 Begin by cutting a thin slice off the bottom of the watermelon so it rests flat and securely on the table. Cut an oval shape out of the top of the watermelon to create an opening. Use a spoon to remove all the watermelon flesh and juice to a bowl (see page 38 for a refreshing watermelon smoothie recipe). Fit the head of lettuce into the hollow watermelon shell, cutting the lettuce as necessary. Stick purple or green kale leaves into the watermelon to cover the lettuce; set aside.

2 Cut the pineapple flowers and cantaloupe flower centers as described on page 7. Slice the unpeeled orange into about 6 wedges. Stick a skewer vertically into each orange wedge. Create the strawberry buds as described on page 16. Place the pineapple flowers, cantaloupe centers, orange wedges and strawberry buds on a large plate; chill in the refrigerator while preparing the chocolate coating.

3 Follow the package directions to melt the chocolate candy coating in the microwave. Depending on the size of your bouquet, melt the entire amount of candy coating or just portions of it. Dip half of a pineapple flower in the chocolate coating; repeat as desired. Dip a few of the strawberry buds in chocolate as described on page 47. Fill the decorating bag with some of the melted chocolate, snip a hole in the end of the bag and decorate the orange wedges with chocolate, moving in a swirling pattern.

4 To make the grape spears, thread 4 or 5 similar-size grapes onto a wooden skewer, starting at the stem-side of each grape and piercing straight through to the bottom end of each grape. Do not pierce all the way through the final grape on each spear, allowing the skewer to remain concealed. For a small-size bouquet, you will need 4 to 6 grape spears. Place the grape spears on a plate and refrigerate to chill.

5 Next, make the melon leaves. Cut the melons into wedges that measure about 1" to 1½" on the widest side. If a rippled effect is desired, cut the melon wedges using a crinkle cutter. Run a knife as close to the outer edge of the melon flesh as possible in order to remove the rind. Insert a skewer vertically into each melon leaf. Refrigerate the melon leaves.

6 Assemble the pineapple daisies as described on page 14, using both plain and chocolate-dipped pineapple flowers. Stick the pineapple daisies into the lettuce-filled watermelon. Arrange the remaining fruit pieces in the bouquet, turning the watermelon often to make sure it is filled evenly on all sides. When you are happy with your bouquet, carefully package it for delivery or return the entire arrangement to the refrigerator until ready to display and serve.

WATERMELON SMOOTHIE

Don't let all that watermelon scooped out of the base of your Feelin' Fruity bouquet go to waste. Blend it into a refreshing smoothie for a cool summer treat, or make a big batch to serve alongside your fruit bouquet!

Ingredients
- 2 C. seedless watermelon chunks
- 1 C. cracked or shaved ice
- ½ C. plain yogurt
- 1 to 2 T. sugar
- ½ tsp. ground ginger
- ⅛ tsp. almond extract

Directions
In a blender, combine the watermelon chunks, ice, yogurt, sugar, ground ginger and almond extract. Process on medium speed until blended and smooth. Pour into 2 to 3 glasses. If desired, garnish the rim of each glass with small strawberries or a watermelon wedge.

Straw-Kiwi Craze

**The perfect combo
for the chocolate
strawberry lover**

You Will Need:

- 4 to 5 kiwis
- 20 to 25 strawberries
- 1 (16 oz.) pkg. microwaveable chocolate candy coating
- 12" disposable decorating bag with optional small tip (#3)
- 20 to 30 (10") bamboo skewers
- 1 head iceberg lettuce
- 1 small bunch purple or green kale or leafy lettuce
- 1 (5½" tall) square container or vase

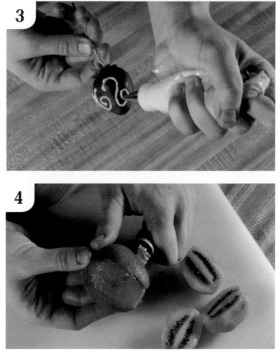

1 Begin by creating the strawberry buds. Rinse the strawberries under cool water and pat dry gently with paper towels. Choose large, full strawberries of a similar size. If desired, remove the stem and leaves from each strawberry, however it is not necessary to do so. Poke the pointed end of a skewer into the stem end of a strawberry stopping before the skewer pierces through the berry; repeat with remaining berries and skewers, then refrigerate.

2 Follow the package directions to melt the chocolate candy coating in the microwave. Depending on the size of your bouquet, melt the entire amount of candy coating or just portions of it. Remove the strawberries from the refrigerator and pat them dry with paper towels. It is preferable to dip cold, dry strawberries. Holding a strawberry bud by the skewer, dip it into the melted chocolate and use a spoon to help coat the strawberry completely.

3 Dip some of the berries entirely in chocolate, but leave most of the berries un-dipped. Working quickly, transfer spoonfuls of the melted chocolate into a plastic decorating bag. If using a tip, fit the tip and/or coupler into the bag before filling. Snip a small hole into the tip of the bag with a scissors. Hold the skewer end of one un-dipped berry in one hand and the filled decorating bag in the other hand. Move the chocolate in a swirling pattern around the berry. Stick the skewers into a sheet of Styrofoam to allow the chocolate to harden.

4 Cut each kiwi in half to make the kiwi flowers. Using a paring knife, gently peel and discard the outer brown skin from each kiwi half. Stick a skewer vertically into one end of each kiwi half, pressing through the kiwi and stopping before the skewer pierces through the other end of the kiwi. Place the kiwi flowers on a plate and refrigerate.

5 Next, prepare the lettuce base. Cut the head of lettuce as necessary to fit easily into the container. Place the lettuce head in the container so the top of the lettuce sits 1" to 2" above the rim of the container. Stick purple or green kale leaves into the container to cover the lettuce. The skewers of fruit added later will hold the kale in place.

6 Once all the coating has dried, begin arranging the bouquet. Place a row of swirled berries around the inside rim of the container. Place a row of kiwi flowers above the swirled berries, followed by a row of chocolate-dipped berries. Top off the center of the bouquet with one large swirled berry. When you are happy with your bouquet, carefully package it for delivery or return the entire arrangement to the refrigerator until ready to display and serve.

GOT MELTED CHOCOLATE?

If you have melted chocolate left over after creating your fruit bouquet, try using it up with one of the following ideas. If the chocolate needs to be re-melted, just heat it in the microwave for 20 seconds and stir; repeat as necessary.

- Pour the chocolate into candy molds to make small treats or favors.
- Using a small pastry brush, paint the melted chocolate onto one side of a clean plastic leaf. Once the chocolate has hardened, peel away the leaf to reveal your textured chocolate leaf; use it to garnish a bowl of ice cream or special dessert.
- Make chocolate cups by painting two to three layers of melted chocolate on the inside of paper cupcake liners or miniature candy liners. Once the chocolate has hardened, peel away the liners. Fill the chocolate cups with pudding, mousse or fresh berries.
- Place a sheet of waxed paper on a flat surface. Using a decorating bag, draw small chocolate letters, numbers and shapes on the waxed paper. Once the chocolate has hardened, carefully lift away the shapes. Or, write the initials of each dinner guest in chocolate and use them to create personalized desserts.

Fruit Loops

Celebrate summertime with disks of chilled cantaloupe, watermelon and honeydew

You Will Need:

- ❏ 1 head iceberg lettuce
- ❏ Container (Sample uses a ceramic pot, 4½" in diameter and 4" deep.)
- ❏ 1 large cantaloupe
- ❏ 1 medium honeydew melon
- ❏ ½ small seedless watermelon
- ❏ Round cookie cutters (1¾", 2", 2¾", 3½")
- ❏ 20 (10") wooden or bamboo skewers
- ❏ 1 small bunch curly parsley

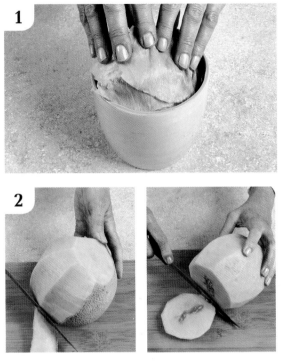

1 Place iceberg lettuce into container, trimming it as needed to achieve a snug fit.

2 Slice off a narrow piece of melon from the stem end. Slice off the cantaloupe rind, removing all green from the orange flesh. Then cut another crosswise slice from end, ½" thick.

3 Cut 2 or 3 (½"-thick) slices from one side of the cantaloupe until center cavity is reached. In the same way, make 2 or 3 (½"-thick) slices on the opposite side of cantaloupe. Repeat to cut ½"-thick slices from remaining 2 sides of cantaloupe.

4 With narrowest side of each melon slice facing up, use cookie cutters to cut out flat disks of cantaloupe. Use the largest cutters that will fit on each slice first; then cut a variety of smaller disks from remaining melon. Arrange cantaloupe disks on a rimmed baking sheet and refrigerate. Discard seeds and reserve any cantaloupe scraps for another use. Prepare and cut honeydew melon as directed in steps 2-4.

5

6

5 Cut watermelon into ½"-thick slices, leaving rind intact. Use cookie cutters of varying sizes to cut out disks from the pink flesh. Arrange watermelon disks on a rimmed baking sheet and refrigerate.

To assemble skewers of fruit, insert the pointed end of a skewer into the edge of a melon disk, gently pressing it through the fruit and stopping about 1" from opposite edge (do not pierce top edge). Thread 1 extra-large or large melon disk on 7 or 8 skewers. Thread 1 or 2 medium and small disks on 7 or 8 skewers. Thread 2 to 5 of the smallest disks on remaining skewers, using a combination of honeydew, cantaloupe and watermelon.

6 To arrange the bouquet, push blunt end of skewers firmly into lettuce base until pieces are straight and secure. Start by inserting largest melon disks in the center of bouquet, trimming skewers as needed to get a variety of heights. (The largest disks generally need shorter skewers for stability.) Insert skewers with next largest disks at the sides and in back of largest pieces, varying the heights. Fill in empty spaces with skewers of smaller disks until bouquet looks balanced. In some spaces, it may be easier to remove melon disks while inserting skewers and then replace the fruit after skewers are secure.

Cover lettuce base with pieces of parsley, tucking them into bouquet with a skewer as needed. Refrigerate bouquet until serving, up to 3 hours.

Berried Treasure Tree

: **This stunning**
: **tree is**
: **dressed to**
: **impress**

You Will Need:

- ❏ Approximately 160 medium to large strawberries
- ❏ Styrofoam cone (Sample is 17" tall with a 4¾" diameter base.)
- ❏ 1 sheet red tissue paper
- ❏ Round toothpicks
- ❏ Base (Sample uses an 8½" round plate.)
- ❏ 8 to 10 sprigs fresh mint leaves
- ❏ ¼ C. white baking chips or bittersweet chocolate chips, optional
- ❏ Small food-safe paintbrush, optional
- ❏ Additional medium and large mint leaves, optional
- ❏ Chocolate Sauce, optional (recipe follows)

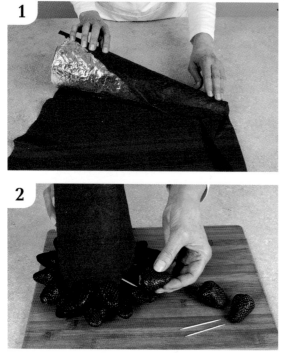

1 Rinse strawberries in cool water and gently remove leaves (but do not cut berries) on all but one large berry (for top of cone); drain well and pat dry. Sort berries in groups of similar sizes, from largest to smallest.

2 Cut off 2" from pointed top of Styrofoam cone. Wrap cone in aluminum foil. Cover foil with tissue paper, folding excess tissue over the top to make a flat surface; tape as needed.

3 Begin assembly around the bottom of cone with the largest strawberries. Push a toothpick horizontally into the cone, about ½" from lower edge, so half of toothpick is exposed. Slide the stem end of 1 large strawberry onto toothpick until it touches cone (side of berry should be even with bottom of cone). Moving around the bottom of cone, insert another toothpick at the same height, about 1" away, allowing enough space for the next berry to fit. Slide a similar sized strawberry

onto this toothpick (strawberries should touch). Fill in the bottom row with berries. In the same manner, place a second row of toothpicks and strawberries above first row, with strawberries just touching to hide most of the tissue paper.

4 Working in rows around the cone from the bottom toward the top, continue to insert toothpicks and strawberries, with largest berries toward the bottom and smaller ones toward the top. When cone is about half covered, transfer to the plate for easier handling. Continue to attach strawberries until cone is covered. Insert a toothpick into the top of cone and slide the leaf end of the reserved strawberry onto toothpick. To finish, insert mint sprigs between berries as desired.

CHOCOLATE LEAVES

To embellish your centerpiece with edible chocolate leaves, melt ¼ cup white baking chips or bittersweet chocolate chips in the microwave and stir until smooth. Set medium and large mint leaves on waxed paper. Dip the paintbrush into melted chocolate and brush generously over leaves; let dry to the touch. Coat leaves with a second layer of melted chocolate and let dry for 30 minutes. Carefully peel off mint leaves and discard. Arrange chocolate leaves among strawberries as desired.

CHOCOLATE SAUCE

Serve warm chocolate sauce alongside the fresh berries, if desired. Place 2 cups semi-sweet or bittersweet chocolate chips in a large bowl; set aside. In a medium saucepan over low heat, combine 1 cup heavy whipping cream, ⅓ cup sugar and ⅓ cup light corn syrup. Bring mixture to a boil, stirring frequently. Remove from heat and pour over chocolate chips in bowl; let stand until chocolate melts. Stir until smooth. Stir in 1½ teaspoons vanilla extract and serve.

Garden Roundup

Fresh fruits star in this flower garden

You Will Need:

- ❏ Melon baller
- ❏ ½ cantaloupe
- ❏ 1 whole fresh pineapple
- ❏ Cookie cutters (2" and 3¼" flowers, 2½" butterfly, 1⅝" star, 1" round)
- ❏ 2 large oranges
- ❏ 1 large red apple
- ❏ Lemon juice
- ❏ 3 kiwifruit
- ❏ 2 green apples
- ❏ 1 bunch red seedless grapes (50 to 60)

- ❏ 1 pt. strawberries (about 25)
- ❏ 2 heads iceberg lettuce
- ❏ Container (Sample uses a 5½" x 10" oblong basket, 3" deep.)
- ❏ 1 yellow apple, optional
- ❏ Fresh parsley
- ❏ 50 to 60 (10" and 12") wooden or bamboo skewers
- ❏ ½ C. white baking chips, optional
- ❏ 1 square chocolate-flavored almond bark, optional
- ❏ Small plastic bag, optional

1 Use the melon baller to cut small and large balls from the cantaloupe; set on a rimmed baking sheet. Cut the pineapple crosswise to make 5 (¾"- thick) disks. Center the large flower cookie cutter over 1 pineapple disk. (Metal cookie cutters are recommended for a clean, even cut.) Press straight down on the cookie cutter, using even pressure. Gently slide the flower shape out of the disk. Repeat to make 2 more flowers. Reserve skins. With the 1" round cookie cutter, cut out the center core of each pineapple flower; discard core.

2 Insert a large melon ball into the hole in each pineapple flower. (Fit should be snug).

3 From the 2 remaining pineapple disks, use cookie cutters to cut out 3 small flowers and 1 butterfly. Cut out small wedges from reserved pineapple skins and any remaining pineapple, cutting through both the skin and flesh. Set all pineapple shapes on the rimmed baking sheet and refrigerate. Cut oranges crosswise into ½"-thick slices. Gently peel off and discard rind; refrigerate orange slices. Cut red apple into 4 crosswise slices, about ⅜" thick. Use the star cookie cutter to cut out the center of each apple slice; discard center. Dip apple slices in lemon juice to prevent browning; set aside.

4

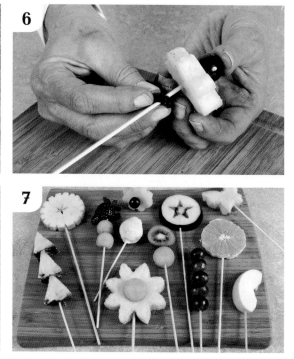

6

5

7

4 Cut kiwifruit into ⅜"-thick slices, making as many as possible. Press the star cookie cutter into the center of the largest slices to cut out 4 kiwi stars. Insert a kiwi star into each red apple slice.

5 Cut green apples into ⅜"-thick slices. Use the center slices with the best star detail. With one point of the small star-shaped cookie cutter, cut out evenly spaced notches around the edge of each slice; carefully remove any seeds. Dip slices in lemon juice.

6 Insert a skewer up through the center bottom of each small pineapple flower, with point sticking out the top; attach a grape to each point. Add a raisin or other dried fruit "stopper" below the fruit to hold flower in place.

7 Push the point of several skewers through 2 to 6 grapes, strawberries and cantaloupe balls without piercing the top fruit. Combine fruits as desired, making both long and short skewers. Carefully insert a 10" skewer halfway through each slice of kiwi, red and green apple and orange until secure. Insert 12" skewers into the edge of each large pineapple flower and butterfly, about ¾ of the way across flower.

8 Begin assembly by placing the largest pineapple flowers, apples and oranges first, trimming skewers as necessary. Fill in around these large pieces with remaining skewers of fruit, placing tallest pieces in back and trimming skewers as needed.

CHOCOLATE-COVERED STRAWBERRIES

To add flavor and elegance, melt ½ cup white baking chips in the microwave and stir until smooth. With strawberries on skewers, dip berries in melted white coating until covered, allowing excess to drip off; set upright in Styrofoam to dry. Melt 1 square chocolate-flavored almond bark and pour warm mixture into a zippered plastic bag. Cut a tiny piece off one corner of bag and pipe fine lines of chocolate over berries; let dry. Insert coated berries in bouquet as desired.

For Your Sweet Side

Ho Ho swirls and fresh fruit make a quick and yummy bouquet

You Will Need:

- 1 whole fresh pineapple
- 8 Ho Ho chocolate cake rolls
- 20 fresh medium strawberries
- 2 bananas (ripe but firm)
- 2 T. lemon juice
- 16 to 20 (10") wooden or bamboo skewers
- 1 (10 oz.) pkg. frozen sweetened strawberries, thawed, optional

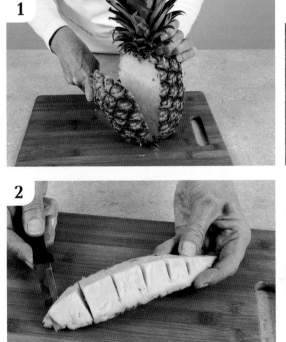

1 Prepare a pineapple "boat" for the base. Set the pineapple upright (leaves up). With a sharp knife, cut through pineapple from top to bottom, in front of the leaves and core, to remove about ⅓ of pineapple. Reserve the large section with leaves; slice remaining section lengthwise into 3 even wedges.

2 Slice each wedge crosswise (through the flesh only) in 1" intervals; cut off the skin to separate the chunks of pineapple. Set pineapple chunks aside and discard skin.

3 Slice each cake roll crosswise into 3 equal pieces; set aside.

4 Cut off the stem end just below the leafy cap of each strawberry; set aside fruit and discard leaves. Peel bananas and cut crosswise into slices about 1" wide. Gently coat banana slices in lemon juice to prevent browning. Drain on paper towels and set aside.

5

6

7

5 Alternately and in any combination, thread pieces of fruit and cake roll onto pointed end of skewers to make the following: 1 skewer with 2 pieces; 6 skewers with 3 pieces; 3 skewers with 4 pieces; 3 skewers with 5 pieces and 3 skewers with 6 pieces. Slide pieces toward the pointed end of each skewer, leaving about 2" of pointed end exposed for pushing skewers into the pineapple base.

6 If necessary, trim off a slice of skin from bottom side of pineapple base so it rests flat. To assemble bouquet, push pointed end of skewers down into the cut side of base until food touches the pineapple and skewers are secure. Insert the smallest skewer first, placing it near the rounded edge near leaves. With the pruning shears, trim off the blunt end of this skewer so about 1" remains exposed.

7 Build the bouquet diagonally across the pineapple by inserting 2 rows of 3-piece skewers behind the smallest skewer; trim off blunt end of each skewer to 1". Continue to insert skewers of increasing length while working toward the back of the bouquet. Trim blunt ends as needed. The tallest skewers should be placed at the back of bouquet. If necessary, make starter holes in the tough core area of the pineapple with another skewer.

Serve bouquet with small bowls of strawberry sauce for dipping, if desired. To make strawberry sauce, place thawed strawberries in a blender container and blend until smooth.

Chocolate Bliss

An eye-catching arrangement of blissfully sweet strawberries

You Will Need:

- ❏ 35 to 40 strawberries
- ❏ 1 (16 oz.) pkg. microwaveable chocolate candy coating
- ❏ 1 (16 oz.) pkg. microwaveable vanilla candy coating
- ❏ Pink gel food coloring
- ❏ 12" disposable decorating bags with optional small tip (#3)

- ❏ Rainbow sprinkles or nonpareils
- ❏ 35 to 40 (10") bamboo skewers
- ❏ 1 head iceberg lettuce
- ❏ 1 small bunch purple or green kale or leafy lettuce
- ❏ 1 clay pot
- ❏ Decorative ribbon and bows

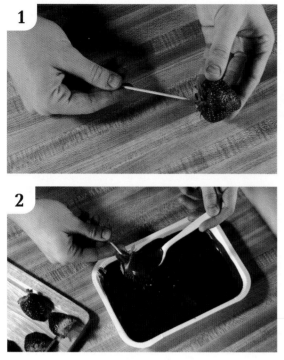

1 Begin by creating the strawberry buds. Rinse the strawberries under cool water and pat dry gently with paper towels. Choose large, full strawberries of a similar size. If desired, remove the stem and leaves from each strawberry, however it is not necessary to do so. Poke the pointed end of a skewer into the stem end of a strawberry stopping before the skewer pierces through the berry; repeat with remaining berries and skewers, then refrigerate.

2 Follow the package directions to melt the chocolate candy coating in the microwave. Depending on the size of your bouquet, melt the entire amount of candy coating or just portions of it. Remove the strawberries from the refrigerator and pat them dry with paper towels. It is preferable to dip cold, dry strawberries. Holding a strawberry bud by the skewer, dip it into the melted chocolate and use a spoon to help coat the strawberry completely.

3 Hold the dipped strawberry over the melted chocolate, allowing any excess to drip off. In order for the chocolate to dry around the strawberries with a smooth finish on all sides, stick the non-berry end of each skewer into a sheet of Styrofoam. To create the sprinkled strawberries, hold a fresh dipped strawberry over a bowl and sprinkle the nonpareils lightly over the coating. Set the coated berries in the Styrofoam to dry completely.

4 Follow the package directions to melt the vanilla candy coating in the microwave. Holding a strawberry bud by the skewer, dip it into the white coating and use a spoon to help coat the strawberry completely. Create 4 to 6 vanilla-coated berries. Stick the skewers into the Styrofoam, allowing the coating to dry.

5 Using a toothpick, add a few drops of the pink gel food coloring to the melted vanilla coating. Quickly stir the coloring into the coating until it turns a light shade of pink. If necessary, add more coloring until your desired shade is achieved. Dip some of the strawberry buds into the pink coating, using a spoon to help coat each strawberry completely.

6 Working quickly, transfer spoonfuls of the melted pink coating (white coating can also be used) into a plastic decorating bag. If using a tip, fit the tip and/ or coupler into the bag before filling it with the coating. Snip a small hole into the tip of the bag with a scissors. To make the dotted berries, hold the skewer end of one chocolate-dipped berry in one hand and the filled decorating bag in the other hand. Dot the pink coating all around the strawberry. Create the swirled berries in the same fashion, moving the pink coating in a swirling pattern around the berry.

7 Next, prepare the lettuce base. Cut the head of lettuce as necessary to fit easily into the pot. Place the lettuce head in the pot so the top of the lettuce sits 1" to 2" above the rim of the pot. Stick purple or green kale leaves into the pot to cover the lettuce. The skewers of fruit added later will hold the kale in place. If desired, wrap a decorative ribbon around the pot.

8 Once all the coating has dried, arrange the berries in the pot. Stick the berries very close together to achieve a full, balanced bouquet. Alternate colors and styles of decorative berries while arranging, turning the pot often to make sure it is filled evenly on all sides. If desired, decorate the bouquet or skewers with small bows made from ribbon. When you are happy with your bouquet, carefully package it for delivery or return the entire arrangement to the refrigerator until ready to display and serve.

Truffle Tower

Delight a chocolate lover with a tower of tasty truffles

You Will Need:

- ❑ Styrofoam cone (Sample is 12" tall with a 3¾" diameter base.)
- ❑ Brown craft paper
- ❑ 3 (12 oz.) pkgs. semi-sweet chocolate chips, divided
- ❑ 2¼ C. sweetened condensed milk, divided
- ❑ ½ tsp. orange extract
- ❑ ½ tsp. raspberry flavoring
- ❑ ½ tsp. almond extract
- ❑ 1 C. sliced almonds, finely ground

- ❑ 7 squares white almond bark, divided
- ❑ Styrofoam sheet covered with waxed paper
- ❑ 7 squares chocolate-flavored almond bark, divided
- ❑ Round toothpicks
- ❑ Zippered plastic bags
- ❑ Red foil or cellophane
- ❑ Base (Sample uses an 8½" plate.)
- ❑ Wide decorative ribbon

1 Wrap Styrofoam cone in aluminum foil. Cover foil with brown paper, folding it over the top and trimming off excess paper; tape as needed and set aside.

Melt 1 package chocolate chips in the microwave, stirring until smooth. Stir in ¾ cup sweetened condensed milk until well mixed. Blend in orange extract. Cover bowl and chill for 45 minutes.

In a clean bowl, melt another package chocolate chips and stir in ¾ cup sweetened condensed milk until blended. Stir in raspberry flavoring. Cover and chill for 45 minutes.

2 In the same manner, melt the last package of chocolate chips and stir in remaining ¾ cup sweetened condensed milk. Add almond extract and stir well. Do not chill, but instead, use the small end of a melon baller to scoop out a ball of dough. With hands, roll dough into a smooth 1" ball.

3 Roll ball in ground almonds until coated; set on a baking sheet. Repeat with remaining dough; cover and chill until assembly.

Shape orange-flavored dough into smooth 1" balls as directed in step 2; place on a baking sheet and refrigerate. Repeat to make 1" balls from raspberry-flavored dough. Place on a baking sheet and chill.

4 Follow the package directions to melt 6 squares white almond bark in the microwave; stir until smooth. Pour melted bark into a deep mug. Working with a few orange-flavored truffle balls at a time (leave remaining truffles in the refrigerator), insert a toothpick about halfway into each ball. Dip each ball into melted white bark to coat; let excess drip back into mug. Stand each truffle upright to dry by inserting the end of its toothpick into waxed paper-covered Styrofoam. Repeat to coat all orange-flavored truffles with white bark.

5 In the same way, melt 6 squares chocolate-flavored bark in the microwave; stir until smooth. Pour melted bark into a deep mug. Working with small batches, insert a toothpick about halfway into each raspberry-flavored truffle ball. Dip balls into melted chocolate bark to coat; let excess drip back into mug. Push toothpicks into waxed paper-covered foam to dry. Repeat to coat all raspberry-flavored truffles with chocolate bark.

6 Melt remaining square white bark in the microwave, stirring until smooth. Pour warm mixture into a zippered plastic bag. Cut off a tiny corner of bag and drizzle white bark back and forth over chocolate truffles. Let dry. In the same manner, melt remaining square of chocolate bark in the microwave, stirring until smooth. Pour into another plastic bag, cut off corner and drizzle over white truffles. Let dry.

7 Wrap 10 to 12 truffles in red foil or cellophane, using tape to secure as needed.

Starting near the base of the cone, make a horizontal starter hole by inserting a toothpick deeply into cone and removing. Insert 1 truffle on its toothpick into starter hole. About 1" to the side of first hole, make another starter hole; insert a second truffle, edges touching. Continue working in rows around cone, alternating flavors and several red truffles, until cone is half covered; transfer to the plate. Continue inserting truffles to cover cone. Lay center of ribbon across top of cone; insert a red truffle and its toothpick through ribbon and into foam.

Pretty in Pink

Chocolate-covered brownies with just enough pink detail to be spot-on

You Will Need:

- ❏ 10 x 15" jelly roll pan
- ❏ 1 (18.3 oz.) pkg. brownie mix*
- ❏ Eggs, vegetable oil and water as directed on brownie mix package
- ❏ Container (sample uses a round cardboard canister, 5" tall and 4½" in diameter.)
- ❏ Styrofoam
- ❏ Pink shredded paper
- ❏ 2 thin rubber bands
- ❏ 2 to 3 (5 oz.) pkgs. Oreo Funstix
- ❏ Wide decorative ribbon
- ❏ Base (such as a 6" cardboard circle or flat platter)
- ❏ Flower-shaped cookie cutter (2½" to 3")
- ❏ 7 (8") white lollipop sticks
- ❏ 1 (16 oz.) pkg. chocolate candy coating
- ❏ ½ C. pink candy wafers
- ❏ Pastry bag fitted with small round tips

* One package yields enough flowers for 2 bouquets.

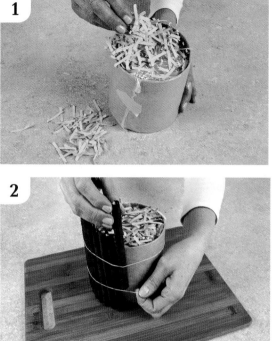

1 Preheat oven to 350°. Spray the jelly roll pan with nonstick cooking spray; set aside. In a large bowl, combine brownie mix, eggs, oil and water as directed on package. Spread batter in prepared pan and bake for 16 to 18 minutes or until a toothpick inserted 2" from edge of pan comes out clean. Cool completely. Wrap waxed paper around container and tape to hold in place; tuck excess over top edge of container. Cut Styrofoam to fit container, ending about 1" below top edge. Wrap foam in aluminum foil, place in container and cover the top with shredded paper.

2 Stretch rubber bands around prepared container near the top and bottom. Carefully insert Oreo Funstix vertically under both rubber bands, one at a time, until container is covered and ends line up with bottom of container. Roll rubber bands toward the middle and tie ribbon around container as desired to hide rubber bands. For added stability, set container on the cardboard circle or platter.

3 Cut out brownie flowers with the cookie cutter, pressing down firmly for clean-cut edges. For easy removal, loosen each flower with a spatula while cutter is still in place and lift from pan; gently press brownie flower out of cutter. Make at least 7 flowers.

4 Gently insert a lollipop stick through the edge of each brownie flower just past its center.

5 Follow the package directions to melt chocolate candy coating in the microwave; stir until smooth. Set a brownie flower on a fork and spoon melted chocolate over the top and sides of flower and over about ¼" of the stick until coated smoothly; shake gently, allowing excess chocolate to drip back into container. Set on a wire cooling rack over waxed paper; let dry for 30 minutes. Repeat to coat all brownie flowers.

6 When dry, spread a thin layer of melted chocolate over the back of each brownie flower; let dry. Re-melt chocolate as needed.

7 Melt pink candy wafers in the microwave according to the package directions; stir until smooth. Spoon warm mixture into a pastry bag fitted with a small round tip. On the front side of each brownie, pipe pink outlines to define "petals" as shown. To make small polka dots, change to a smaller round tip and make small dots on petals as desired. Let dry.

8 Plan placement of brownie flowers, using the photo as a guide. Make starter holes in the foam base with a toothpick before inserting sticks. Trim off 3" from the stick of the front center flower; insert stick into foam base so flower rests low in container. Cut off 1" from sticks for the next 2 flowers and insert into foam just in back and to the sides of front flower. Arrange remaining flowers, working from front to back and pushing sticks into foam as far as necessary for a balanced bouquet.

Whole Kit & Caboodle

**It all stacks up
to sweet fun–
Scotcheroos, Kit
Kats and M&Ms**

You Will Need:

- ❑ 9 (10") wooden or bamboo skewers
- ❑ 9 large yellow gumballs
- ❑ 9" round pan
- ❑ 8" or 9" square pan
- ❑ 12 C. Special K cereal
- ❑ 3 C. peanut butter
- ❑ 2 C. light corn syrup
- ❑ 2 C. sugar

- ❑ 2 C. milk chocolate chips
- ❑ 2 C. butterscotch chips
- ❑ Base (Sample uses a 13" round glass platter, bottom side up.)
- ❑ 6 (3.92 oz.) pkgs. snack size Kit Kats (about 48)
- ❑ 1 (42 oz.) bag M&Ms
- ❑ Wide rick-rack trim

1 Push the pointed end of 1 skewer into the center of each gumball; set aside. Line round and square pans (at least 1½" deep) with waxed paper; set aside. Pour cereal into a large bowl; set aside.

In a large saucepan over medium heat, combine peanut butter, corn syrup and sugar. Cook until sugar is dissolved, stirring occasionally. Pour mixture over cereal in bowl and stir until well combined. Spread cereal mixture evenly in prepared pans and press firmly.

Using the waxed paper, remove cereal mixture from the 9" round pan. Center the cereal disk upside down on the base to form the bottom layer. Peel off waxed paper and discard.

2 Using the waxed paper, remove the cereal mixture from the square pan. Place the cereal square upside down on a cutting board. Peel off waxed paper and discard. To make patterns, draw and cut out 1 (6") and

1 (3") circle on parchment paper. Fit patterns on top of the cereal square as shown in photo and use a sharp knife to cut around each circle to make 2 more round layers; set aside.

3 In a microwave-safe bowl, combine chocolate and butterscotch chips and melt in the microwave; stir until smooth. Spread an even layer of chocolate mixture over the top of the 9" layer.

4 Center the 6" layer on the first layer and frost the top of the second layer. Place the 3" layer on top of that; frost the top and side of the third layer. Reserve remaining chocolate mixture for step 6.

5 Immediately place Kit Kats vertically* around the side of the top layer until covered, pressing to affix candy to the chocolate mixture. Cut Kit Kats to fit, if necessary.

6 Attach Kit Kats around the middle and bottom layers by placing a dab of reserved chocolate mixture on the bottom 1" of the back side of candy and pressing to fasten securely*.

7 Pour M&Ms over each cereal layer, filling to the top of the Kit Kats.

8 Press the blunt end of each gumball skewer into the top layer, varying the heights as desired. Attach rick-rack trim around middle of bottom layer.

* Be sure to line up the Kit Kat bars so that the words, "Kit Kat", run the same direction on each layer.

Pie to Go

Sweet little fruit pies tucked into an eat-on-the-go bouquet

You Will Need:

- ❏ Styrofoam
- ❏ Container (sample uses a ceramic pot, 5½" tall and 3¾" in diameter.)
- ❏ Shredded tissue paper
- ❏ 1 (14.1 oz.) pkg. ready-to-use pie crust (2 crusts)
- ❏ Round cookie cutters (2" to 2½")
- ❏ 12 white lollipop and/or cookie sticks (4", 6", 7" or 8")
- ❏ Fruit pie filling or preserves of choice (Sample uses blueberry and strawberry pie filling and apricot preserves.)
- ❏ Milk, divided
- ❏ Sugar
- ❏ ¾ C. powdered sugar
- ❏ Pastry bag fitted with a small round tip
- ❏ Zippered plastic bags, optional
- ❏ Narrow ribbon to match filling colors

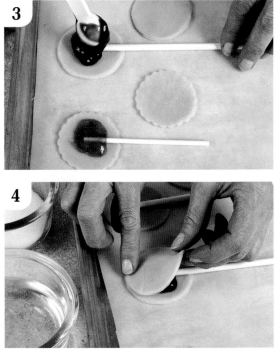

1 Line a large baking sheet with parchment paper. Preheat oven to 400°. Cut Styrofoam to fit into container, leaving 1" of space at the top. Wrap foam in aluminum foil and press into container. Cover top with shredded tissue paper.

2 Let pie crusts stand at room temperature for 15 minutes. Handling 1 crust at a time, gently unroll on a flat surface. With cookie cutters, cut out matching pairs of circles, cutting as many as will fit.

3 Place pairs of crust circles on prepared pan. Press 1 lollipop or cookie stick on 1 circle of each pair, about ¾ of the way across circle. Use different lengths of sticks, placing the shortest and longest sticks on the smallest pies. Place about a teaspoonful of filling or preserves in the center, covering the end of stick and leaving about ⅜" uncovered around outside edge.

4 With a fingertip dipped in water, dampen the outside edge of pastry circle. Place the matching circle on top and press edges together with a fingertip. With fingers, press crust against stick.

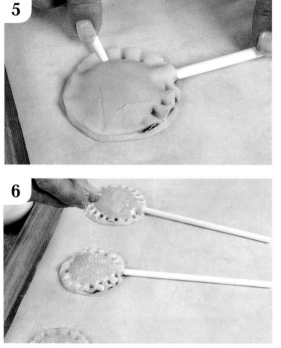

5 Press the end of a short lollipop stick around the edge of crust to seal and create an indented pattern.

6 Brush the top of pies with milk and sprinkle with sugar.

Bake for 15 to 17 minutes or until golden brown; remove from oven. Carefully remove any filling that has seeped from the pies. Cool pies completely. Use fresh parchment paper to bake each batch of pies.

7 Whisk together powdered sugar with enough milk to make a thick smooth icing. Place icing into the pastry bag fitted with a small round tip and pipe lines across as many pies as desired. Let stand at least 15 minutes.

8 Cut a 12" piece of ribbon for each pie. (Match ribbon color to filling, if desired.) Tie a small snug bow around stick under each pie.

To arrange, press sticks into base, starting with largest pies in the center and alternating colors as desired. Fill in front and back with smaller pies using photo as a guide.

Minty Blooms

: **Eating a tree never**
: **tasted so good**

You Will Need:

- ❏ 3 squares chocolate-flavored almond bark
- ❏ 5 to 6 (10 oz.) pkgs. chocolate-covered cookies (such as Keebler Grasshopper cookies)
- ❏ Round toothpicks
- ❏ 6 large sheets green tissue paper (or another color)
- ❏ Decorative scissors
- ❏ Styrofoam cone (Sample is 17" tall with a 4¾" diameter base.)
- ❏ Base (Sample uses a ceramic pedestal, 4" tall and 6" in diameter.)

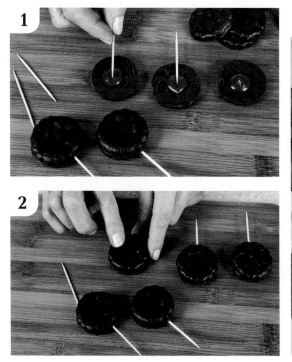

1 Melt almond bark in the microwave according to the package directions; stir until smooth.

Line up a few cookies on a flat work surface, bottom side up. Spoon a small amount of melted bark on the center of each cookie and press a toothpick into melted bark, about halfway across cookie.

2 Quickly set a second cookie on top of toothpick and bark, edges even, to make sandwich cookies; toothpick should stick out about 1½". Hold in place several seconds until set. Repeat to make approximately 100 sandwich cookies. Set aside and let dry completely.

3 Make a pattern by cutting out a 4½" square piece of paper. On a sheet of tissue paper, trace around the pattern as many times as possible. Stack sheets of tissue paper together and use decorative scissors to cut through the layers as traced. (You will need about 100 squares.)

Fold each tissue paper square as shown on the pattern to make a "pleated pocket." To do this, first fold the square along diagonal dotted line to within ¾" of the opposite sides. With the fold at the bottom, bring the lower left and right corners toward the center until folded edges meet in the middle and sides are lined up. Crease well to create a square pocket with opening at the top.

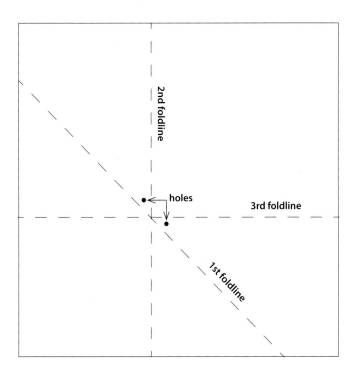

2nd foldline

holes

3rd foldline

1st foldline

Pleated Pocket Pattern

**Enlarge square to 4½" and cut 100 squares
from tissue paper.**

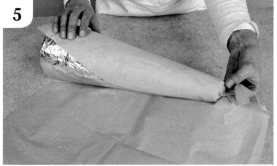

4 With a plain toothpick, make 2 starter holes through the folded tip in each pocket as shown on pattern. Remove toothpick. Insert sandwich cookie, pushing the point of its toothpick through both starter holes so cookie is inside the pocket.

5 Cut off 2" from top of Styrofoam cone. Wrap cone in aluminum foil. Cover foil with tissue paper, twisting the excess tissue paper at the top into a tuft.

6 To assemble, press the toothpick of each cookie and pocket horizontally into the foam to make a row around the bottom of cone, placing cookies close together. Place pleated side of each pocket facing up. Insert another row above first row, staggering cookies between previous ones. Continue to insert rows of cookie pockets, working from bottom to top until cone is covered.

7 Remove final cookie from its tissue pocket; insert toothpick and cookie into the tissue tuft on top of cone. Arrange the tissue pocket behind cookie in tuft as desired. Carefully lift cone and set it on pedestal before serving.

Sunny-Side Up

Shed a little sunshine with this cookie and cupcake bouquet

You Will Need:

- Muffin pan
- Paper cupcake liners
- 1 (18.2 oz.) pkg. yellow cake mix
- Eggs, vegetable oil and water as directed on cake mix package
- Styrofoam (Sample uses a disk, 1" thick and 5¾" in diameter and a ball, 6" in diameter.)
- Container (Sample uses a metal bucket, 5½" deep and 7" in diameter.)
- Filler (Sample uses brown shredded paper.)
- 18 wooden or bamboo skewers
- 18 (2 oz.) plastic cups*
- 9 Oreo cookies (or more as needed)
- 2 C. prepared white decorator icing
- Gel or paste food coloring (yellow)
- Pastry bag fitted with a medium star tip

1 Preheat oven to 350°. Line muffin cups with paper liners; set aside. Prepare cake batter as directed on cake mix package. Fill liners about ½ full with batter. Bake as directed on package; set aside to cool completely.

2 Place Styrofoam disk in bucket, firmly pressing down until level and securely lodged in bucket. Cut a thin slice from one side of foam ball and place flat side on foam disk in bucket. Fill gap between foam ball and bucket with filler. Place some filler over foam ball.

3 Trim skewers to 3½" to 4" lengths. Poke pointed end of skewer through the bottom center of a plastic cup. Insert blunt end of skewer into foam ball, positioning so the side edge of cup rests on top edge of bucket. Push skewer deeply into foam until the bottom of the cup rests against the foam ball and the pointed end of the skewer protrudes about 1" through the center of cup. Continue around perimeter of bucket and then work upward until foam ball is covered with skewers and plastic cups.

4 Separate the 2 halves of each cookie, removing the cream centers. Tint icing with yellow food coloring as desired. Frost cupcakes with a thin layer of icing. Carefully place a cupcake in each plastic cup, pushing it onto skewer. Immediately press 1 cookie half in the center of each frosted cupcake.

5 Place remaining icing into the pastry bag. Pipe a row of short icing petals around each cookie by squeezing the bag, then lifting and "laying" the icing out and upward, ending the petal halfway between the edge of cookie and the edge of cupcake. Make a second row of petals, starting at the outer edge of previous petals and ending at edge of cupcake, positioning petals between previous petals. Tuck extra filler between cupcakes as desired.

* Or cut 18 (8 oz.) Styrofoam cups to 1" or 1½" in height.

Stuck on My Honeydew

Fruit and cheese kababs add fun to any party

You Will Need:

- Melon baller
- ½ honeydew melon (cut crosswise), seeded
- ½ cantaloupe, seeded
- 1 small head iceberg lettuce
- 2 (½"-thick) crosswise slices from a whole fresh pineapple
- Small metal cookie cutters (1½" heart, 1" square, 1" round, 1¼" diamond)

- 3 (12 oz.) blocks cheese, 1" thick (Sample uses Cheddar, Colby-Jack and mozzarella.)
- 1 bunch red seedless grapes (45 to 50)
- 1 bunch green seedless grapes (45 to 50)
- 5 (10") wooden or bamboo skewers
- 75 to 80 (4") party picks
- Large plate (Sample uses a 10" round glass plate.)

1 With a melon baller, cut small and large balls from the flesh of honeydew melon, making as many as you can; set balls on a rimmed baking sheet and refrigerate until assembly. With a large spoon, scrape out remaining flesh, leaving a melon shell about ½" thick. Pat shell dry with paper towels; set aside. Cut additional small and large balls from cantaloupe flesh; place on rimmed baking sheet and refrigerate.

2 Peel off outer leaves of lettuce and trim head as needed until it fits snugly inside melon shell.

3 With lettuce inside shell, carefully slice lettuce so its cut edge is level with cut edge of melon.

4 To cut a pineapple heart, place cookie cutter on 1 pineapple slice, with point toward core and curved edges near pineapple skin. (Metal cookie cutters are recommended for a clean, even cut.) Press straight down on the cookie cutter, using even pressure. Remove pineapple heart from cutter. Repeat to cut 6 to 7 hearts from each pineapple slice. Place hearts on a rimmed baking sheet and refrigerate until assembly.

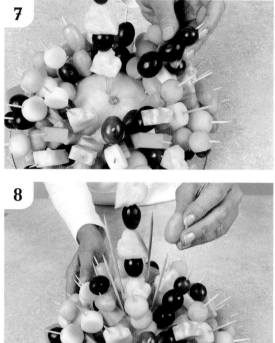

5 Cut through the 1" thickness of each block of cheese using the square*, round and diamond cookie cutters to make "plugs" of each shape. With a sharp knife, slice plugs in half to ½" thickness. Cover cheese until assembly.

Just before assembly, pat fruits dry with paper towels. Trim 1 skewer to 8" long. Insert the point through 3 alternating pineapple hearts and grapes; set aside.

6 Using the 4" picks, make skewers of fruit and/or cheese, alternating pieces as desired. Avoid placing melon and cheese on the same skewer. Make half of the picks with 3 items and remaining picks with 2 items. Grapes and cheese shapes may be skewered lengthwise or crosswise. Allow at least ½" of exposed pick at each end: one end to poke into the base and the other end for guests to hold.

7 Set melon/lettuce base on the plate, cut side down. With a skewer point, make a starter hole in center top of melon, avoiding the stem; press reserved 8" pineapple heart/grape skewer into hole. Insert a row of 18 to 20 (3-item) picks around the bottom of melon, about ½" from cut edge. Repeat with a row of 2-item picks, 1" above first row, staggering them between previous picks. Insert additional rows of 2- and 3-item picks to cover melon, but leave about 1" of open space remaining around tall center skewer.

8 Trim 3" to 4" off blunt end of remaining 4 skewers. Make starter holes in open space around top of melon; push trimmed end of skewers into holes to desired height. Thread fruit and cheese onto exposed skewers, sliding pieces down toward melon. Fill any open space with remaining short picks. Serve promptly or refrigerate for up to 1 hour before serving.

On a Roll

Tiny cinnamon rolls and candied pecans– perfect for snacking or brunch

You Will Need:

- No-knead bread dough (recipe on page 126)*
- 1 egg white
- ½ C. plus 2 T. brown sugar, divided
- ¼ tsp. vanilla extract
- 4 C. whole pecans
- 3½ T. sugar, divided
- 1½ tsp. ground cinnamon, divided
- Container (Sample uses a 5" round tin, 2" deep.)
- Sheet of Styrofoam (1⅛" thick)
- 40 (3") cinnamon sticks
- Low-temperature glue gun
- Raffia
- ¼ C. butter, melted
- Unflavored dental floss or string
- 30 (10") wooden or bamboo skewers
- Buttercream frosting (recipe on page 83) or 1 C. canned frosting
  * You may also purchase 28 to 30 small snack-size cinnamon rolls.

1 Prepare No-Knead Bread Dough with vegetable oil according to recipe on page 126. Let rise for 2 hours. Meanwhile, prepare candied pecans to cover base. Preheat oven to 300°. Line a baking sheet with waxed paper and spray with nonstick cooking spray; set aside. In a medium mixing bowl, beat egg white on high speed until stiff peaks form. Stir in ½ cup brown sugar and vanilla until smooth. Stir in pecans until coated. Spread on prepared baking sheet and bake for 15 minutes. In a small bowl, mix 1½ tablespoons sugar and ½ teaspoon cinnamon. Remove pecans from oven and stir to separate. Sprinkle with cinnamon-sugar; toss to coat. Return pan to oven for 3 minutes. Cool completely. (Use about 1 cup pecans for bouquet; serve remaining nuts on the side or reserve for another use.)

2 When ready to bake rolls, preheat oven to 350°. Line a baking sheet with aluminum foil and spray with nonstick cooking spray; set aside.

Snip off a ball of prepared dough the size of a large orange (about ½ pound). Sprinkle with flour, stretch and shape dough into a smooth ball. On a floured surface, roll out to a thin 7 x 12" rectangle. In a small bowl, stir together remaining 2 tablespoons sugar, 2 tablespoons brown sugar and 1 teaspoon cinnamon. Spread half the melted butter over dough. Sprinkle with half the sugar mixture.

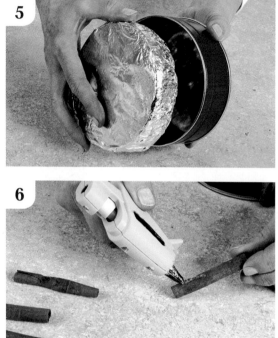

3 Starting at one long edge, roll up dough tightly to make a log; pinch long edge to seal. Use floss to cut dough into ¾"-wide slices (14 to 15 slices). Place slices on prepared baking sheet and flatten to ½" thickness. If desired, pinch opposite edges to make a few "leaf" shapes. Repeat with another piece of dough. (For a larger bouquet, make additional rolls and increase amount of frosting.)

4 Bake rolls for 15 to 18 minutes or until golden brown. Remove from pan and let cool.

5 Cut Styrofoam to fit container, with top resting just below top edge of container. Wrap foam in aluminum foil and place in container.

6 With a glue gun, attach cinnamon sticks vertically to the side of container, placing ends even with bottom and lining up sticks until covered. Tie raffia around the outside.

7 To assemble bouquet, insert pointed end of skewers into one edge of each cinnamon roll without piercing the top (unless placing more than 1 roll on a skewer). Trim skewers as needed to get different lengths. Insert blunt end of longest skewers in the center area of foam base first. Arrange medium skewers at angles pointing outward from the center. Place shorter skewers toward the front and back of arrangement to fill bouquet. When you like the arrangement, pipe or spread Buttercream Frosting (recipe on page 83) on approximately 12 cinnamon rolls. If preferred, slide those rolls off their skewers, frost them and then carefully replace frosted rolls on skewers. Extra frosting may be served with the bouquet.

8 Cover base with prepared candied pecans before serving.

BUTTERCREAM FROSTING

- 3 T. butter, softened
- Dash of salt
- ½ tsp. vanilla extract
- 1 T. half & half
- ¼ c. sifted powdered sugar

In a small bowl, beat together butter, salt, vanilla, half & half and powdered sugar until smooth and creamy. Spread frosting on cinnamon rolls with a knife or place frosting in a pastry bag fitted with a round tip and pipe frosting on rolls as desired. (Frosts 12 to 18 rolls)

SHRIMP FILLING

(Try this alternate filling for Pinwheel Palooza on page 119.)

- 1 ripe avocado
- 4 oz. cream cheese, softened
- ¼ C. ketchup
- 1 T. prepared horseradish
- 1 tsp. finely grated lemon zest
- 2 T. lemon juice
- ½ tsp. chili powder
- 5 (10") whole wheat or flour tortillas
- 3 C. shredded spinach leaves
- ⅔ C. smoked almonds, chopped
- 1 (4 oz.) can tiny shrimp, drained

Pit and dice avocado as directed on page 106. In a medium bowl, mash avocado flesh. Mix in cream cheese, ketchup, horseradish, lemon zest, lemon juice and chili powder until smooth and well-blended. Spread mixture over one side of tortillas. Top with a layer of spinach. Sprinkle evenly with almonds and shrimp. Roll up tortillas tightly and refrigerate for 30 minutes before slicing into pinwheels. (Fills 5 tortilla rolls)

Autumn Splendor

Pumpkin-flavored cookies match the all-around festive tone of this bouquet

You Will Need:

- 2 C. prepared white decorator icing, divided
- Gel or paste food coloring (yellow, gold, orange, brown, red)
- Pastry bag fitted with medium round and leaf tips
- Yellow nonpareils
- Pumpkin sugar cookie dough (recipe on page 87)
- Cookie cutters (1½" round, several 3" to 4" leaves, 2½" acorn)

- Drinking straw, optional*
- Cookie icing (recipe on page 87)
- 1 to 2 squares white almond bark
- Small pumpkin (sample is 7" tall and 6½" in diameter.)
- Candle (sample is a brown pillar candle, 3" tall and 3" in diameter.)
- Base (sample is a branch wreath, 18" in diameter with a 5" opening.)

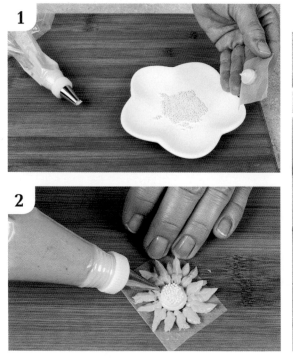

1 Tint ½ cup decorator icing bright yellow with food coloring. Tint remaining 1½ cups decorator icing bright orange.

Place yellow icing into the pastry bag fitted with the round tip. Cut waxed paper into 20 (1½") squares. To pipe the yellow center of each flower, squeeze icing from the bag onto the middle of a waxed paper square until the center of the flower is ⅜" to ½" high. Pick up the waxed paper square and immediately dip the yellow center into nonpareils.

2 Place orange icing into another pastry bag fitted with the leaf tip. To pipe the orange petals, squeeze icing from bag, lifting as pressure is released from bag and "laying" the icing petals from the yellow center toward the outside. Continue around the center as shown, petals touching. In the same manner, pipe 2 shorter rows on top of the first row, beginning at yellow center and staggering each row so the petals fall between those in the previous row. Set aside. Repeat to make 20 flowers. Cover loosely and let stand overnight or for up to 5 days.

3 Prepare Pumpkin Sugar Cookie Dough using the recipe on page 87. Roll out chilled dough to a thickness of ¼" to ⅜". Cut out about 10 large leaves, 10 medium leaves, 6 to 8 small leaves, 10 acorns and 30 small rounds. (Cut hanging holes before baking if desired*.) Bake cookies at 375° for 9 to 13 minutes or until lightly browned on bottom. Cool completely on a wire rack. Serve any extra cookies alongside the bouquet or save for another use.

Prepare Cookie Icing using the recipe on page 87 or use additional decorator icing. Divide icing between 4 bowls. To each bowl, add food coloring to create desired shades of red, orange, yellow and brown. Frost leaves as desired, dragging knife to make a leaf-like texture on top. Frost acorns brown. Let icing dry at least 2 hours.

4

5

4 Follow the package directions to melt 1 square almond bark in the microwave, stirring until smooth. Using a metal offset spatula, carefully remove an icing flower from waxed paper square and attach it to a small round cookie with a dab of melted bark, pressing gently on the yellow center. Decorate 20 round cookies with icing flowers. Let dry. Reserve remaining bark.

Break off pumpkin stem. Set candle on top of pumpkin and trace around it with a pencil. With a sharp knife, cut along traced line and remove top. Scoop out seeds. Set candle into carved hole to check fit; trim opening as needed for easy removal of candle. Set aside. Crumple aluminum foil to fill pumpkin; set candle into hole on top of foil and adjust height.

To assemble, cover top of wreath with plastic wrap. Set pumpkin in center opening of wreath. Arrange leaf, acorn and plain round cookies around pumpkin on plastic, alternating shapes and colors. Arrange 9 or 10 flower cookies on top of leaf cookies.

5 Re-melt reserved almond bark in the microwave; stir until smooth. Attach flower cookies around pumpkin opening by placing a dab of melted bark on the back of a cookie and pressing it against pumpkin until set. Repeat to make a row of about 10 flowers.

*To hang cookies from pumpkin, use a straw to poke a hole in cookies before baking. After baking, cooling and frosting, thread ribbon or jute through hole, tie a knot and attach to cut edge of pumpkin with a toothpick.

PUMPKIN SUGAR COOKIES

(Makes about 36)

¾ C. butter, softened

1 C. sugar

½ C. pumpkin puree

½ tsp. vanilla extract

2½ tsp. pumpkin pie spice

3 C. flour

1 tsp. baking powder

½ tsp. salt

In a large mixing bowl, beat butter on medium speed until creamy. Add sugar and beat until light and fluffy. Add pumpkin, vanilla and pie spice, beating until well blended. In a separate bowl, stir together flour, baking powder and salt. Add flour mixture to pumpkin mixture and beat until well mixed and a stiff dough forms. Cover and chill for at least 1 hour. Then follow cutting and baking directions on page 85 to make Autumn Splendor.

COOKIE ICING

1½ T. meringue powder

2 C. powdered sugar

1 tsp. clear vanilla extract

½ tsp. butter flavoring

3 T. warm water

Low-fat milk

Gel or paste food coloring (autumn colors)

In a medium mixing bowl, combine meringue powder, powdered sugar, vanilla, butter flavoring and water; beat on medium speed until smooth and fluffy, about 4 minutes. Stir in 1 to 2½ tablespoons milk, a little at a time, to reach desired spreading consistency. Then follow the directions on page 85 to tint and frost the pumpkin cookies used in Autumn Splendor.

Savory

Too-Cute Tulips, page 97.

Taco Blooms, page 104.

Skinny Dippin', page 101.

Pinwheel Palooza, page 119.

Escape to Capri, page 107.

Veggie Delight

A gratifying
selection
of veggies
perfectly
arranged for
dipping

You Will Need:

- 3 to 4 green, yellow and red bell peppers
- 1 small bunch cauliflower
- 1 small bunch broccoli
- 1 cucumber
- 1 zucchini
- 5 to 7 large carrots
- 5 to 7 large radishes
- 10 to 12 cherry tomatoes
- 1 bunch green onions
- Crinkle cutter
- Vegetable coring tool
- Small flower-shaped cookie cutter
- 45 to 60 (10") bamboo skewers
- 1 head iceberg lettuce
- 1 small bunch purple or green kale or leafy lettuce
- 1 medium basket

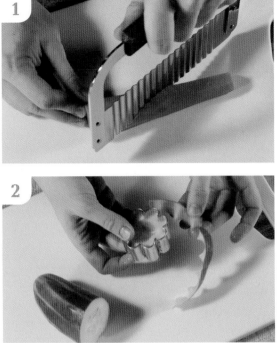

1 Begin by making the carrot spears. Peel and wash each carrot, then cut off both ends of the carrot to make two flat ends. Using the crinkle cutter, cut each carrot through the center at a diagonal, creating two carrot pieces. Stick a skewer into the flat end of each carrot piece. Separate the cleaned broccoli and cauliflower into small florets. Stick a skewer into the bottom of each floret; set aside the vegetable pieces in the refrigerator.

2 To make the cucumber flowers, slice the cleaned and dried cucumber into ½"-thick rounds. To cut a flower, center the flower-shaped cookie cutter over a cucumber round. Press straight down on the cookie cutter, using even pressure. Stick a skewer into a cucumber flower, pressing from the flat bottom side, through the center, to the top side of the flower. Slide one cherry tomato onto the exposed end of the skewer.

3 Next, create the bell pepper flowers. Wash and pat dry 1 or 2 green bell peppers. Cut the peppers in a zig-zag pattern horizontally around the center. Carefully pull the two sides apart and remove the inner membrane and seeds. Use a few of the cucumber flowers as centers for the bell pepper flowers. Stick a skewer through the bottom of the pepper, through a cucumber flower, then into a cherry tomato.

4 Use the coring tool to cut a hole entirely through a radish. Remove the core, leaving the outer radish as a tube. With the coring tool still in the radish, cut vertical lines around the radish tube, stopping about halfway down the side. Stick a cherry tomato snuggly inside each radish tube. Press the radish flower onto a skewer by sticking it into the tomato from the bottom side.

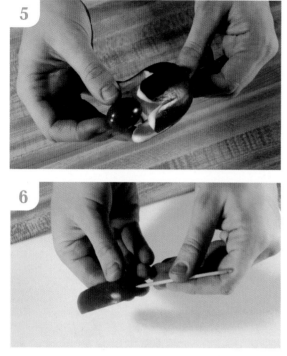

5 Wash and pat dry the zucchini. To make the zucchini flowers, cut the zucchini into 2" segments. Run a knife vertically between the outer zucchini peel and inner flesh to create the petals, stopping about 1½" down the side of the zucchini piece; repeat to make 5 petals. Carefully remove the inner flesh in the center of the petals, leaving a ½" base of zucchini intact. Stick a skewer up through the bottom of the flower and top with a cherry tomato.

6 Cut the yellow and red bell peppers into thin wedges that are the length of the pepper and about ¾" wide in the center. Carefully slide the peppers onto skewers, piercing once at the pointed end of a pepper wedge and poking gently into the other pointed end.

7 Make thin green onion leaves by running a knife through each onion to make two halves; cut the ends into points. Next, prepare the lettuce and kale base as described in previous arrangements.

8 Finally, fill the bouquet with the vegetable flowers and leaves. When you are happy with your bouquet, carefully package it for delivery or return the entire arrangement to the refrigerator until ready to display and serve.

CREAMY DILL DIP

Serve or give your Veggie Delight bouquet with this delicious dill dip. Those vegetables will disappear in the blink of an eye!

Ingredients

4 oz. reduced-fat
   cream cheese, softened
½ pkg. dry ranch
   dressing mix
2 T. skim milk
1½ tsp. dried dillweed or
   1 T. chopped fresh dill

Directions

In a food processor, combine the cream cheese, ranch dressing mix, milk and dillweed. Process on medium speed until blended and smooth. Store the dip, tightly covered, in the refrigerator until ready to serve. Transfer the dill dip to a serving dish. Place on the table alongside the bouquet and encourage guests to dip their veggies.

RANCH VEGGIE DIP

The crowning detail for your Regal Relish bouquet is this tasty ranch veggie dip. The dip can be made ahead of time and stored in the refrigerator for up to 10 days.

Ingredients

1 C. reduced-fat mayonnaise
½ C. reduced-fat sour cream
½ tsp. dried chives
½ tsp. dried parsley
   flakes
½ tsp. dried dillweed
¼ tsp. ground garlic
¼ tsp. onion powder
⅛ tsp. salt
⅛ tsp. pepper

Directions

In a bowl, mix together the mayonnaise, sour cream, chives, parsley, dillweed, ground garlic, onion powder, salt and pepper; mix until blended and smooth. Store the dip, tightly covered, in the refrigerator until ready to serve. Transfer the ranch dip to a serving dish. Place it on the table alongside the bouquet and encourage guests to dip their veggies.

Regal Relishes

A vegetable
arrangement fit for
the royal court

You Will Need:

- ❏ 20 to 25 cherry tomatoes
- ❏ 1 each yellow and red bell peppers
- ❏ 5 to 7 long celery ribs
- ❏ 1 large bunch broccoli
- ❏ 1 (16 oz.) bag rippled carrot chips
- ❏ 5 to 7 radishes
- ❏ 25 to 30 (10") bamboo skewers
- ❏ 1 head iceberg lettuce
- ❏ 1 small bunch purple or green kale or leafy lettuce
- ❏ 1 small to medium oval basket

1 Begin by breaking each skewer in half so you have approximately 50 to 60 (5") skewers. Short skewers are desirable since the vegetables sit close to the base. Wash and pat dry the tomatoes. Stick one short skewer gently into the stem end of each cherry tomato, stopping before the skewer pierces through the tomato. Set the tomato buds on a plate and chill in the refrigerator while preparing the remaining pieces.

2 After washing and patting dry the yellow and red bell peppers, cut them into wedges that are the length of the pepper and about ¾" wide in the center. Carefully slide the peppers onto skewers, piercing once at the pointed end of a pepper wedge and poking gently into the other pointed end; refrigerate.

3 Rinse and pat dry the celery ribs. Cut both ends of a celery rib into a point, then cut the rib in half in the middle creating two pointed celery pieces. Repeat with the remaining celery ribs. Gently slide a skewer into the flat end of each celery point, stopping before the skewer pierces through the celery. Refrigerate the celery points.

4 Separate the cleaned broccoli into small florets. Stick a skewer into the bottom of each floret; set aside in the refrigerator. To make the carrot spears, choose 10 to 16 long and thick carrot chips from the bag. Gently slide the pointed end of a small skewer into the thickest end of a carrot chip; set aside in the refrigerator.

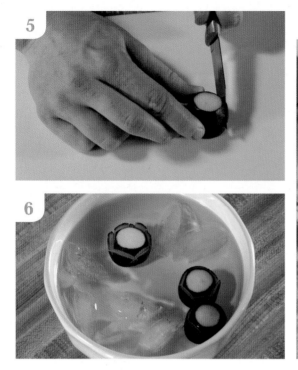

5 To make the radish rosettes, wash and gently pat dry the radishes. Cut off both ends of each radish to make two flat sides with the white inner radish exposed. Use a paring knife to cut ½" petals along the side of each radish. Place the radish rosettes in a bowl of ice water to help open up the petals, as shown.

6 Next, prepare the lettuce base. Cut the head of lettuce as necessary to fit easily into the basket. For a small to medium oval-shaped basket, cut about 2" from both sides of the lettuce head. Use the cut-off pieces to fill the bottom and sides of the basket, then place the lettuce head in the basket so the top of the lettuce sits 1" to 2" above the rim of the basket. Stick purple or green kale leaves into the basket to cover the lettuce.

7 Arrange the vegetable skewers in sections. Create two rows of tomato buds along the basket rim on one long side. Stick the celery and carrot spears in rows around both short sides of the basket. Create two rows of pepper wedges along the other long side of the basket. Fill in the center with broccoli florets and radish rosettes. When you are happy with your bouquet, carefully package it for delivery or return the entire arrangement to the refrigerator until ready to display and serve.

Too-Cute Tulips

Tiptoe through the tulips, asparagus and green onions for crunchy goodness

You Will Need:

- ❑ 1 (16 oz.) pkg. large red radishes (about 20), room temperature
- ❑ 2 bunches medium green onions
- ❑ 6 to 10 fresh asparagus spears
- ❑ ½ head red cabbage
- ❑ Container (Sample uses a glass vase, 3½" in diameter and 9" tall.)
- ❑ 15 (12") wooden or bamboo skewers
- ❑ 10 to 15 (10") wooden or bamboo skewers

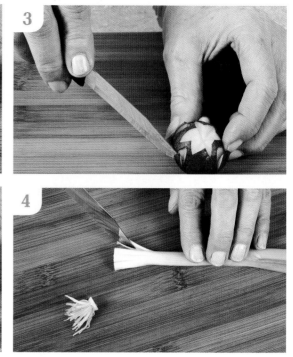

1 With a small sharp knife, slice off the stem end of a radish so it will rest flat on a cutting board. Cut a V-shaped wedge from center top of radish by slicing the first side of the "V" about ¼" deep and then making an opposing cut until root can be removed.

2 Cut out 2 more V-shaped wedges from top of radish, positioning them like an "X" over the first wedge, to make a 6-pointed star.

3 To cut "petals," insert knife point about ⅛" below a red peak. Make one shallow slice down the radish under the peak, angling knife toward the center like half of another V-shape while following the line of the peak. About ¼" from the bottom of radish, gently withdraw knife to stop the cut. To make the other half of the same petal, re-insert knife tip so it intersects the top of the first cut. Make another shallow, angled slice down radish under the peak on the other side to complete

the "V", stopping near the bottom as before. Do not connect the bottom cuts or the petal will fall off radish. Petals should be a bit loose to the touch. Repeat process to make 1 petal under each peak. Gently bend petals outward and place radish in ice water for 1 or 2 hours or overnight. Repeat steps 1-3 to make 15 radish tulips. (For convenience, make radish tulips the day before assembly.)

4 To make green onion frills, slice off root of each onion. Make 3 thin lengthwise cuts through the white bulb end of onion, about 1¼" long. Roll onion a quarter turn (to uncut side) and slice once or twice more. Trim frills to 4" lengths. Place frilled pieces in ice water for at least 1 hour; reserve green stems for step 7.

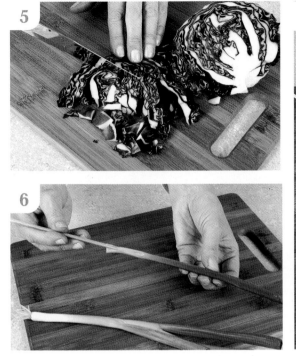

5 Trim 1" off thick ends of asparagus spears. To parcook, wrap spears in wet paper towels and microwave for 1½ minutes. Let cool slightly, unwrap and rinse in cool water; place in ice water.

Slice and coarsely chop cabbage. Place in vase, filling about ⅔ full.

6 Cut off bulb end of remaining onions and reserve for another use. Separate the long green stems. Gently slide 12" skewers into either end of larger onion stems to cover. Slide 10" skewers into smaller stems.

7 Slide 10" skewers into thick end of asparagus spears as far as possible without splitting spears. Slide 10" skewers into cut end of onion frills (toward frilled end) until secure.

8 Arrange the longest skewers in the vase (for tulips), pushing blunt ends into cabbage until secure. Press radish tulips onto skewer points and arrange "flowers", trimming skewers as needed until bouquet looks balanced. Work from the back of bouquet toward the front.

9 Add asparagus spears and onion frills to complete the bouquet, trimming skewers as needed. Bouquet can be refrigerated for up to 2 hours before serving*.

* Just before serving, spritz or brush radishes with water.

Skinny Dippin'

A garden of crisp vegetables and dip–a colorful low-cal snack or appetizer

You Will Need:

- 10 large red radishes
- 6 to 8 stalks celery, divided
- 8 to 10 fresh asparagus spears
- 1 bunch green onions
- 1 stalk fresh broccoli
- 3 large bell peppers (Sample uses 1 yellow, 1 green and 1 red.)
- 4 to 5 medium carrots, peeled
- 1 pt. red grape tomatoes, divided (about 20)
- Round toothpicks, broken in half
- 1 medium cucumber
- Melon baller
- 2 dressings or dips of choice (such as ranch or honey mustard)
- Narrow platter (Sample uses a ceramic platter, 14" long and 6½" wide.)
- Green kale, optional

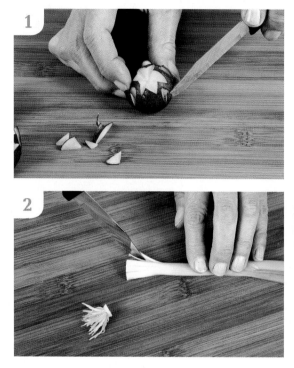

1 Cut and chill radish tulips following the directions on page 98 or radish wheels following directions on page 123. If desired, make and chill celery curls from 2 stalks of celery according to directions on page 123.

2 Prepare green onion frills following the directions on page 98.

Parcook and chill asparagus spears according to directions on page 99.

Cut off each floret from the broccoli stalk; cover with damp paper towels and refrigerate.

3 To prepare bell pepper "pots," use a sharp knife to cut out the stem and core of each pepper; discard. Carve around top edge of peppers, following ridges to create a scalloped or zigzag edge. Carefully remove seeds and white membranes inside; rinse out hollow shells and drain on paper towels.

Cut remaining celery into 4" to 4½" lengths. Split the wide pieces into narrower sticks. Cut carrots to the same length, using the thickest end of each one. Split carrots in half lengthwise.

4 Insert a toothpick half into one end of 10 wide and 12 narrow celery sticks. Insert a toothpick half into the wide end of each carrot stick. Attach a radish tulip or wheel to the toothpick on the wide celery sticks and a grape tomato on the narrow celery sticks. Attach a broccoli floret to the toothpick on each carrot stick.

5 Cut 2 (2") lengths from the center of the cucumber. With a melon baller, hollow out both pieces, leaving 1" of flesh intact to form the bottom of each pot. Drain or pat dry with paper towels. Fill pots with dressing or dip.

Set peppers on the platter, trimming away bumps on the bottom as needed so pots will stand up. Fill yellow pepper with radish-celery tulips; fill green pepper with broccoli-carrot sticks and prepared onion frills. Fill red pepper with tomato-celery sticks and chilled asparagus spears. Set cucumber pots on platter and garnish with kale, celery frills and remaining tomatoes as desired. Fill cucumber pots with dressing or dip.

Taco Blooms

Let the fiesta begin with this colorful layered dip and tortilla chips

You Will Need:

- ❏ 1 (10") sun-dried tomato basil flour tortilla (or more)
- ❏ 1 (10") garden spinach herb flour tortilla (or more)
- ❏ Leaf-shaped cookie cutter (3" to 4")
- ❏ 2 tsp. olive oil
- ❏ Salt to taste
- ❏ 1 (16 oz.) can refried beans
- ❏ 1 (1 oz.) pkg. taco seasoning mix
- ❏ 1 ripe avocado*
- ❏ ½ (1 oz.) pkg. guacamole seasoning mix
- ❏ 1⅓ C. sour cream, divided
- ❏ Pastry bag fitted with large open star tip
- ❏ 6 oz. cream cheese, softened
- ❏ Large platter (Sample uses a 13" charger.)
- ❏ 1¼ C. chunky salsa, divided
- ❏ 1 C. shredded Cheddar cheese, divided
- ❏ 1 Roma tomato, chopped and drained
- ❏ 4 green onions, sliced
- ❏ Scoop-type tortilla chips, divided
- ❏ 1 (2.25 oz.) can sliced black olives, drained

1 Preheat oven to 400°. Line a large baking sheet with parchment paper; set aside.

Stack tomato basil and spinach herb tortillas together, edges even. Press a leaf cookie cutter firmly through both layers to cut out 2 leaf shapes; repeat to make about 14 leaves. Arrange leaves in a single layer on prepared baking sheet and brush tops with oil. Bake for 4 to 5 minutes or until edges just begin to brown. Remove from oven and sprinkle with salt; let cool on pan.

In a medium bowl, stir together refried beans and taco seasoning mix; let stand for 15 minutes to blend flavors. In a small bowl, mash avocado flesh and stir in guacamole seasoning until well blended; cover and refrigerate at least 15 minutes. Place ⅓ cup sour cream into a pastry bag fitted with a large open star tip; reserve in refrigerator for piping. Whisk together remaining 1 cup sour cream and cream cheese until blended; set aside.

2 Reserve ⅓ cup bean mixture to fill scoops. Spread remaining bean mixture in an 8" circle over the center of platter. Spread sour cream mixture over beans.

3 Spread avocado mixture over creamy layer. Top with about 1 cup salsa followed by ¾ cup Cheddar cheese, tomato and green onions; press lightly to hold in place.

4 Spoon 1 teaspoon reserved bean mixture into about 15 tortilla chips. Top each chip with a sprinkling of remaining Cheddar cheese. Spoon ½ teaspoon of remaining salsa over cheese.

5 With reserved pastry bag, pipe a sour cream flower on each filled chip. Top with a sliced olive.

6 Arrange chip "flowers" over layered mixtures on platter.

7 Arrange tortilla leaves around edge of platter. Serve promptly with remaining tortilla chips.

*AVOCADO PREP

Cut avocado lengthwise around the seed. Twist halves apart to expose pit. Poke a knife edge into the pit and twist to remove. Cut through avocado flesh in both directions without cutting the skin. Flex skin slightly and scoop out diced flesh with a spoon.

Escape to Capri

A taste of Italy–tortellini, mozzarella cheese, tomatoes, black olives and herbed breadsticks

You Will Need:

- ❑ No-Knead Bread Dough (recipe on page 126) *
- ❑ Olive oil
- ❑ Grated Parmesan cheese
- ❑ Coarse salt
- ❑ Italian seasoning
- ❑ 8 oz. fresh mozzarella cheese
- ❑ 1 green bell pepper, cored and seeded
- ❑ 30 frozen cheese tortellini, plain and/or spinach flavor (about 1½ cups)
- ❑ 16 to 20 large pitted black olives, drained (about 3 oz.)
- ❑ 1 bunch fresh basil leaves, rinsed and patted dry
- ❑ 1 pt. red grape tomatoes
- ❑ 1 pt. yellow cherry tomatoes
- ❑ 1 (14 oz.) can artichoke hearts, drained and sliced, optional
- ❑ 16 to 20 (10") wooden or bamboo skewers
- ❑ Container (Sample uses a 3 x 3½" rectangular glass vase, 7" deep.)
- ❑ Italian Dipping Sauce (recipe on page 109)

1 Prepare No-Knead Bread Dough with olive oil according to recipe on page 126. Let rise for 2 hours.

2 Preheat oven to 375°. Line a baking sheet with aluminum foil and brush with olive oil; set aside. Snip off a ball of dough the size of a large orange (about ½ pound). Sprinkle with flour, stretch and shape dough into a smooth ball. On a floured surface, roll out to a 7 x 10" rectangle. Brush with olive oil; sprinkle with Parmesan cheese, salt and Italian seasoning to taste.

3 With a pizza cutter, slice the length of dough into ¼"-wide strips.

4 Arrange strips on prepared baking sheet, stretching slightly; twist or shape one end of each strip as desired so finished breadsticks are 8" to 10" long. Bake for 10 to 12 minutes or until golden brown. Cool completely.

Cut mozzarella cheese into ½" to ¾" cubes; set aside. Cut green pepper into 1" pieces; set aside. Cook tortellini in boiling water as directed on package. Rinse in cool water, drain and set aside.

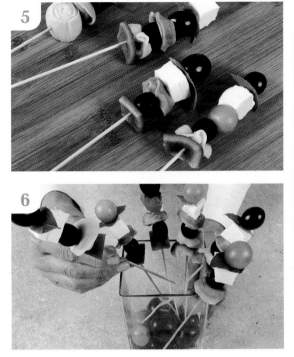

5 To assemble bouquet, slide a piece of green pepper onto the pointed end of each skewer, followed by 1 or 2 tortellini, a black olive, cheese cube and tomato. Add sliced artichoke hearts, if desired. Alternate the order of items but always place the green pepper "stopper" first to anchor other foods. Top most of the skewers with tomatoes; top remaining skewers with cheese.

6 Fill the vase partway with some of remaining tomatoes. Arrange skewers in vase, starting around the edges first. Place sticks at an angle toward the center, between tomatoes without piercing them. Add more tomatoes to vase. Arrange remaining skewers to fill center section of vase.

7 Place breadsticks between skewers until bouquet looks full. Serve promptly with Italian Dipping Sauce to drizzle over skewers and breadsticks.

ITALIAN DIPPING SAUCE

In a small bowl, whisk together ¼ cup olive oil, ¼ cup balsamic or red wine vinegar, 1 tablespoon chopped fresh basil, ¼ teaspoon dry oregano, 1½ teaspoons finely minced garlic, ¼ teaspoon coarse salt and dash of pepper.

For a quicker dipping sauce, use bottled Italian salad dressing.

Oriental Garden Bundles

A crunchy new twist on shrimp-filled spring rolls

You Will Need:

- ❏ 10 thin 6½" egg roll/spring roll wrappers (from a 16 oz. pkg.)
- ❏ Toothpicks
- ❏ Parchment paper
- ❏ 3 T. light soy sauce, divided
- ❏ 2 T. rice vinegar or white wine vinegar
- ❏ 6 T. apple cider
- ❏ ½ tsp. grated gingerroot
- ❏ 20 large, fully-cooked frozen shrimp, thawed

- ❏ 1 medium cucumber, peeled, seeded and chopped
- ❏ 1 medium carrot, julienned*
- ❏ 2 green onions, chopped
- ❏ 2 T. stir fry sauce
- ❏ 2 T. creamy peanut butter
- ❏ 2 C. shredded leaf lettuce
- ❏ ¼ C. chopped fresh cilantro, plus whole leaves for garnishing
- ❏ Container (Sample uses a 5" square metal pot, 5" deep.)
- ❏ Sweet and sour sauce, optional

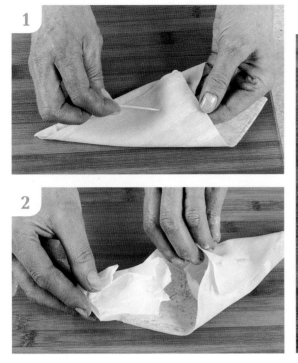

1 Preheat oven to 400°. Line a baking sheet with parchment paper; set aside.

Working with one egg roll wrapper at a time, roll wrapper into a cone shape, overlapping two opposite corners in front, with one corner at the top and the point of the cone at the bottom. Fasten overlapping layers together with a toothpick.

2 Crumple small pieces of parchment paper and gently tuck inside cone to hold it open. Set cone on a paper plate and microwave on high for 30 to 45 seconds or until firm. Let cool slightly and remove parchment paper. Reuse crumpled paper for additional cones.

3 Transfer cones to prepared baking sheet and spray generously with nonstick cooking spray. Bake for 2 to 3 minutes or until light golden brown around edges. Cool slightly before removing toothpicks; then cool completely.

In a medium bowl, stir together 2 tablespoons soy sauce, rice vinegar, apple cider and gingerroot.

Remove tails from shrimp and rinse with cold water. Chop 10 shrimp and place in bowl with soy sauce mixture. Add cucumber, carrot and green onion; toss to coat. Marinate in refrigerator for 15 minutes, stirring several times. Reserve remaining whole shrimp for garnishes.

4 In a small bowl, combine stir fry sauce, peanut butter and remaining 1 tablespoon soy sauce; whisk until smooth. Spread a spoonful of peanut sauce inside each baked cone.

Drain marinated shrimp mixture, reserving sauce for serving. Fill each cone with a portion of the lettuce, chopped cilantro and shrimp mixture.

5 Top with more lettuce, cilantro leaves and 1 reserved whole shrimp.

6 Place crinkled aluminum foil in the bottom of container as needed. Arrange cones in container, gently pressing ends into foil for support and placement. Serve with sweet and sour sauce and/or remaining soy sauce marinade for dipping.

*TO JULIENNE CARROTS

Peel the carrot and cut off a thin lengthwise slice to make a flat side. Cut into 2" lengths. Place pieces flat side down and cut into thin lengthwise slices. Stack several slices together and cut again to make thin matchstick strips.

Bloomin' Tomatoes

Creamy fillings in cherry tomatoes for bite-size appetizers

You Will Need:

- 35 to 40 red cherry tomatoes
- 6 oz. cream cheese, softened, divided
- ½ C. shredded smoked Gouda cheese, room temperature
- 2 T. butter, softened
- 1 T. milk
- ½ tsp. steak sauce
- Pastry bags fitted with large open star tips
- ½ ripe avocado, pitted, peeled and diced
- 1½ T. basil pesto
- 1 tsp. lemon juice
- 1 head iceberg lettuce
- Container (Sample uses a ceramic bowl, 7½" in diameter and 3" deep.)
- 1 small bunch green kale
- Toothpicks

1 With a sharp knife, cut a thin slice off the top of each tomato. Cut around the inside to loosen flesh.

2 With a small spoon or melon baller, carefully scoop out seeds and soft flesh to make a hollow cavity. Set tomatoes, cut side down, on a baking sheet lined with paper towels; let stand for 30 minutes to drain.

To make smoked cheese filling, in a small mixing bowl, combine 4 ounces cream cheese, Gouda cheese and butter. Mash to blend. Add milk and steak sauce; beat on medium speed until fluffy. Spoon mixture into a pastry bag fitted with a large open star tip and set aside.

3 To make avocado-basil filling, in another small bowl, combine avocado, remaining 2 ounces cream cheese, pesto and lemon juice. Mash well and whisk until smooth. Spoon filling into another pastry bag fitted with a large open star tip; set aside.

Set lettuce into container and trim off bottom slightly so top of lettuce mounds about 2" above rim. Tuck pieces of kale around the edges, between container and lettuce.

4 Insert a toothpick into the center top of lettuce until ¾" of pick remains visible. Gently press the bottom of 1 tomato onto toothpick, hollow side up. Insert a row of toothpicks into lettuce around center tomato and attach a tomato to each pick. Working in a circular pattern, insert additional toothpicks into lettuce and attach remaining tomatoes to cover lettuce.

5 Pipe fillings into tomatoes, alternating colors as desired*. Serve promptly or refrigerate for up to 2 hours before serving.

* To stuff all tomatoes with a single flavor of filling, double the appropriate filling ingredients.

BLT Bouquet

The bacon-
lettuce
and-tomato
sandwich just
got better

You Will Need:

- ❏ No-Knead Bread Dough (recipe on page 126)*
- ❏ Vegetable oil
- ❏ Round oven-safe bowl (6" to 7"in diameter)
- ❏ 1 egg
- ❏ 20 slices white bread
- ❏ Flower-shaped cookie cutters (3", 2")
- ❏ 28 to 34 (10") wooden or bamboo skewers

- ❏ 10 slices thick-cut bacon
- ❏ 6 (⅛"-thick) slices provolone or American cheese, optional
- ❏ 1 pt. yellow cherry tomatoes (about 20)
- ❏ ½ head iceberg lettuce
- ❏ Mayonnaise
- ❏ 2 pts. red grape tomatoes (about 45)
- ❏ Large plate (Sample uses a 9" round ceramic plate.)

1 Prepare No-Knead Bread Dough with olive oil according to recipe on page 126. Let rise for 2 hours.

To make 1 round loaf, use half of prepared dough (about 1 pound). Dust dough with flour and shape into a ball, stretching the top smooth and tucking it under the bottom. Oil an oven-proof bowl and place dough in bowl, smooth side down. Cover with lightly-oiled plastic wrap; let rest in a warm place for 1 hour. (If dough is refrigerated, let it rest for 1½ hours.)

Preheat oven to 350°. Uncover bowl and bake bread for 35 minutes or until lightly browned and firm. Meanwhile, whisk egg with 1 tablespoon water. Remove bread from bowl and invert onto an ungreased baking sheet; brush top (the side shaped like the bowl) with egg mixture. Return to oven to bake for 10 minutes more. Let bread cool completely before assembling bouquet.

2 Decrease oven temperature to 375°. With the 3" cookie cutter, cut flowers from 20 slices of bread. Use a skewer to poke a small starter hole in the center of each flower. Bake flowers on an ungreased baking sheet for 12 minutes or until crisp and light golden brown. Cool completely.

Cut bacon strips crosswise into 3 pieces (about 3" long). In a large skillet, fry bacon on both sides until almost crisp; drain on paper towels.

3 With the 2" cookie cutter, cut flowers from provolone and/or American cheese, if desired. Set aside.

4 Cut lettuce into small wedges. Spread mayonnaise on the center of each bread flower.

5 To make BLT skewers, slide a small grape tomato on the pointed end of a skewer followed by a bread flower, cheese flower (if desired), 1 or 2 pieces of bacon and lettuce wedge. Finish with another tomato but do not pierce the top.

Make 7 or 8 skewers of yellow cherry tomatoes, placing 2 or 3 tomatoes on each skewer without piercing the top tomato; set aside.

6 For the base, place round loaf of bread on the serving plate. To assemble bouquet, trim 6 to 8 BLT skewers to 5" lengths; insert these skewers into the loaf around lower edge. Trim another group of BLT skewers to 6½" lengths and insert into bread above first row. Insert remaining long BLT skewers into top section of bread, trimming skewers as needed for a balanced bouquet. Fill in empty spaces with yellow tomato skewers. Serve promptly.

* Prepare loaf of bread at least 4 hours ahead of time or the day before assembling bouquet.
* You may also purchase a 1-pound round loaf of dense bakery or artisan bread.

Pinwheel Palooza

Hearty tortilla rolls, pretty enough to eat

You Will Need:

- Sheet of Styrofoam, 2" thick
- Container (sample uses a 7 x 9" metal platter, 1½" deep.)
- Tacky mounting putty
- ⅓ C. mayonnaise
- 2 cloves garlic, minced
- 3 (10") sun-dried tomato basil flour tortillas
- 1 C. fresh spinach leaves, stems trimmed
- 6 thin slices deli roast beef
- 6 thin slices provolone cheese
- 1 large tomato, thinly sliced
- 1 C. chopped fresh broccoli
- 4 oz. cream cheese, softened
- 1 tsp. dried dillweed
- 1½ tsp. lemon juice
- ¼ tsp. paprika
- ¼ tsp. garlic salt
- Pepper to taste
- 1 medium carrot, grated
- ¼ C. finely chopped green bell pepper
- ⅓ C. frozen peas, thawed
- 3 (10") garden spinach herb flour tortillas
- 40 wooden or bamboo skewers and cocktail picks (4" to 10" long)
- 1 small bunch green kale

1 Cut Styrofoam to fit container and wrap in aluminum foil. Attach foam base to bottom of container with mounting putty; set aside.

2 In a small bowl, mix mayonnaise and garlic; spread thinly on one side of each tomato basil tortilla to within 1" of edges. Top with spinach leaves and a layer of roast beef (2 pieces per tortilla). Arrange provolone cheese and tomato slices over center of meat. Roll up tortillas tightly and set on a plate, seam side down. Refrigerate for 30 minutes.

Microwave broccoli with 2 tablespoons water for 1½ minutes or until slightly tender. Rinse in cold water, drain and set aside.

3 In a medium bowl, mix cream cheese, dillweed, lemon juice, paprika, garlic salt and pepper. Spread a thin layer on one side of each spinach herb tortilla to within 1" of edges. Sprinkle with an even amount of carrot, bell pepper, peas and broccoli. Roll up tortillas tightly and set on a plate, seam side down. Refrigerate 30 minutes.

Trim 1" off each end of tortilla rolls; discard. Slice remaining rolls crosswise to make pinwheels, about 1" wide. Cut approximately 7 pinwheels from each tortilla roll.

4 Cover foam base with kale, using toothpicks as needed to hold in place.

5 Make 4 or 5 double pinwheels by inserting the pointed end of a 10" skewer through 2 contrasting pinwheels, without piercing the top edge of upper pinwheels. Make single pinwheels of shorter lengths, trimming 1" to 3" off blunt end of 10" skewers as needed. If using 4" cocktail picks for the pinwheels in front, push the picks all the way through, from top to bottom with the "handle" on top.

6 Push blunt end of skewers into the base, arranging the double pinwheels across the center first. Place next-longest skewers at angles, pointing outward from each double pinwheel, to create 3 or 4 "bunches." Arrange shorter skewers vertically or at angles in empty spaces. Finish by placing shortest picks around the edges. Refrigerate for up to 3 hours before serving.

VARIATIONS

Use whole wheat or flour tortillas for pinwheels. Add these to the bouquet as a third color or use them in place of colored tortillas.

Prepare and use other fillings as desired, such as the Shrimp Filling on page 83.

Deli Delight

A basket full of crowd-pleasing meat, cheese and veggie hors d'oeuvres

You Will Need:

- 30 round thin deli slices ham, turkey and hard salami*
- 20 thin slices provolone, Colby-Jack and/or American cheese*
- 2 stalks celery, ends removed
- 6 radishes
- 25 to 30 (10") wooden or bamboo skewers
- 2 to 3 medium carrots, peeled
- Crinkle cutter
- Wood and/or plastic toothpicks
- 2 medium cucumbers
- Melon baller
- 4 yellow or red cherry tomatoes, optional
- 15 medium pitted black olives, drained
- 8 to 10 large stuffed green olives, drained, divided
- 12 to 15 red grape tomatoes
- Container (Sample uses a 9" round basket, 3" deep.)
- 2 heads iceberg lettuce
- 1 small bunch green kale
- Flower-shaped cookie cutter (3")
- Spreadable chive and onion cream cheese, room temperature
- 6 to 8 sweet gherkin pickles, drained
- 6 to 8 whole cobs baby corn, drained
- 6 pretzel rods

* Allow meat and cheese to stand at room temperature for 30 minutes for easier handling.

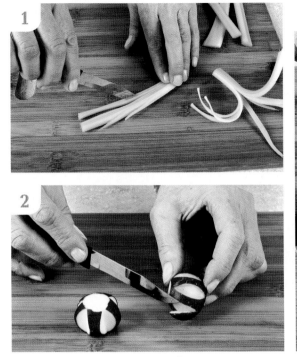

1 To make celery curls, cut celery stalks into finger lengths; split pieces in half lengthwise. With a sharp knife, make parallel lengthwise cuts through each piece, starting about 1" from an end and placing cuts very close together. Chill in ice water for 2 hours or until curled.

2 To prepare radish wheels, slice off stem and root of each radish, leaving a small white circle on the top and bottom. Cutting at an angle, slice out small V-shaped wedges of red skin, running between top and bottom of radish; remove wedges. Space wedges evenly to show white stripes. Poke the point of a skewer into the edge of each radish wheel; cover with damp paper towels.

Cut thickest end of carrots into 5" lengths. With a crinkle cutter, slice each length into 4 even spears. Poke a toothpick into the large end of each carrot spear; wrap in damp paper towels.

3 Cut off 1¼" from both ends of cucumbers; reserve center part of cucumber for another use. With a melon baller, remove insides of cucumber ends to make shells. With a sharp knife, cut out 5 evenly spaced triangles from the edge of each shell to create "flower petals." Round off the corners of each petal and trim out excess flesh. Fasten a cherry tomato in the center by inserting a toothpick from bottom of shell into tomato without piercing the top. Cover with damp paper towels.

Make several skewers of black olives; make other skewers of green olives with grape tomatoes, reserving some for meat and cheese flowers. Cover with damp paper towels.

4 Line basket with waxed paper. Place both heads of lettuce in basket, cutting 1 head as needed for a snug fit. Lettuce should mound above top of basket slightly. Arrange kale over lettuce.

5 Push the point of a skewer into one end of the following center items: pickle, corn, green olive or grape tomato. Place the skewered item on the center of a meat/cheese stack and fold lower edges over each other to form a cone shape with skewer sticking out the bottom.

6 With the cookie cutter, cut half of cheese slices into flower shapes. Bouquet flowers can be made with various combinations of meat and cheese and a small amount of cream cheese spread between the layers. Stack 1 or 2 meat slices with 1 cheese slice, staggering top edges. (Cheese may be on the top or bottom.)

7 Fasten overlapping layers in front with a toothpick. Make about 18 skewers this way.

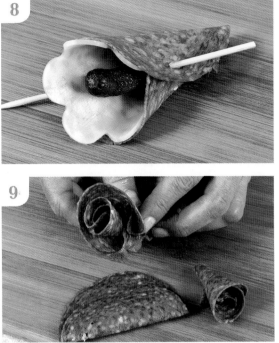

8 For remaining 6 to 8 flowers, wrap the meat/cheese layers around an unskewered center item and shape the cone, but push a skewer point through the whole flower at an angle to hold it together. Cover all cones with waxed paper to prevent drying.

9 Fold 1 piece of salami in half, about ¾" off center. Roll it into a small cone, cut edges up. Wrap a second slice of salami around cone so upper edge flairs out like a flower, folding up bottom edge to enclose cone and finish rosette; fasten with a toothpick.

10 Gather prepared skewers. Begin bouquet assembly by inserting skewers of meat and cheese flowers into base, trimming skewers as needed so flowers rest low in bouquet. Place them in different directions so arrangement is attractive from all sides.

11 Place cucumber flowers low in bouquet, pressing toothpicks into base. Fill open spaces of bouquet with carrot spears, radish wheels, pretzel rods** and skewers of olives and tomatoes. Drain celery curls, insert toothpicks and add to bouquet as desired. Serve promptly.

** Break off one end of each pretzel rod and gently twist a toothpick into broken end so pretzel can be inserted into base more securely.

NO-KNEAD BREAD DOUGH

(Yield: 2 pounds dough)

Use this recipe to make breadsticks, mini cinnamon rolls and round or standard loaves of bread. Prepare the basic dough below and then follow specific directions on bouquet pages to shape and bake as desired. Dough may be refrigerated for up to 5 days before shaping and baking.

1 (¼ oz.) pkg.
granulated yeast

1½ tsp. salt

1 egg

¼ C. honey

2½ T. olive oil or
vegetable oil

3 C. flour

½ C. whole wheat flour

1 In a large bowl, stir together 1 cup lukewarm water, yeast, salt, egg, honey and oil until blended. Mix in both flours until incorporated. Cover loosely and let rise at room temperature for about 2 hours.

2 Shape the dough immediately as desired and bake as directed, or cover and refrigerate for up to 5 days. To remove the quantity of dough needed for a recipe, simply dust with flour and cut off amount needed with kitchen shears or knife. Then refer to the following bouquet pages for shaping and baking. Refrigerate remaining dough and use it within 5 days.

Use this dough to:

- Shape and bake a round artisan loaf for BLT Bouquet on page 116.
- Shape and bake herbed breadsticks for Escape to Capri on page 107 or to garnish Deli Delight on page 122.
- Shape and bake mini cinnamon rolls for On a Roll bouquet on page 79.

Recipe Index by Ingredient